ALE

THERE IS A WAR

HOW TO WIN THE BATTLE OVER THE MASTERS OF THE SOUL

FORWARD BY **NATHAN FINOCHIO**

AFTERWORD BY **DAVID CAMPBELL**

CONTENTS

Title Page ---------- i

Copyright ---------- ii

Contents ---------- iii

Foreword ---------- iv

Part 1 - Hear the War

1 - South Beach ---------- 2

2 – Born For More ---------- 18

3 – No Sleep Till... ---------- 31

4 - Let it Rain ---------- 47

5 - Lions of Distractions ---------- 59

6 - The Door is Open ---------- 71

Part 2 - Heal the Soul

7 - Breaking Free ---------- 84

8 – Press Reset ---------- 99

9 – The Deception of Pride ---------- 118

10 - Don't Settle There ---------- 134

11 - Moving Forward ---------- 148

12 - Glory Days ---------- 163

Afterword ---------- 178

FOREWORD

I find it fascinating that most people are willing to believe in the idea of a God—an all-powerful Being that observes human affairs and works miracles—but don't consider the idea of Satan, a devil, or a personal evil leading a cosmic rebellion against this God.

The Bible teaches that the devil is not God—he is not omniscient (all-knowing), omnipresent (everywhere at once), or omnipotent (all-powerful). Perhaps there are two challenges to common thoughts on evil: that it has far too much reach, or that it doesn't exist in an incarnated and organized sense.

Both assumptions—that evil is remotely as strong as the Creator or, conversely, that it is not effective at all—can set us up for failure.

On the one hand, we have the first category—the "Devil can read my mind" category. People in this group tend to blame demonic activity for every problem in their lives. They believe the reason they are overweight or can't find a parking spot is because Satan himself is after them. I tell most people that the Devil probably doesn't even know their name—like, don't flatter yourself.

This type of thinking underestimates the ability of the Spirit of God. It makes the blood of Christ seem impotent and fruitless, when in actuality, it is the most powerful element in the universe.

If you are in Christ, the Devil is going to be terrified of you.

On the other hand, the second category lives in ignorance of the fact that Satan and his cohorts have influence. The New Testament calls the Devil and his minions the "rulers of this world" or "principalities and powers." Their focus is on deceiving humanity into idolatry, creating a sense of possibility and purpose that actually results in utter chaos and hopelessness.

It's like selling people fake tickets to a concert.

You spend hundreds, perhaps thousands, on two tickets to see so-and-so, and everything leading up to the show is preparation and bliss. The night finally arrives, you're both dolled up and looking one hundred, and as you go to scan what you believe to be valid passes, security informs you that your tickets are invalid.

That's what idolatry is: a god that doesn't deliver. For a while, it feels like the purchase was a success, but when it is actually tested, it fails.

The work of the rulers of this age, the prince of the air, is to create a sham and scam system that captures your focus, attracts your worship, and enlists your participation in an environment that ultimately dumps people into disaster. The preamble is real—the tailgate is enjoyable—the pre-gaming is about as good as it gets. But the tickets are fake, and they lead to death and destruction.

The promise of sex is intimacy and satisfaction, but in the words of Mick Jagger, there is no satisfaction, no matter how much porn or apocalyptic hookups you amass.

The promise of drugs and parties is ecstasy—a higher place—an escape, but it never delivers properly. You just wind up in therapy or in a gym somewhere eating clean.

You find another idol—the idol of your health. "I feel better," you think. You're progressing. But what you've done is put your hope in something that absolutely nobody in the history of the world has ever escaped alive—life.

Because everybody dies, and when your health begins to deteriorate—that thing you put all your hope and faith in to "feel better"—you begin to panic and crumble under the weight of anxiety, because your god is on fire and the tickets aren't working.

Sex is good, and so is working out—but these are meant to be a servant, not a master.

The way Satan destroys you is not by making you a toothless vagabond living under a bridge—although that could happen. The way he gets you is by selling you fake tickets to paradise through his system of idolatry, making you worship an inferior god that you somehow think will get you into the concert.

All of us have a sense of destiny—that our lives are supposed to be moving somewhere. That's actually innate. Yes, we have a beginning and an ending here on earth, but our spirits correctly tell us that this is absurd.

Consider death. It's absurd. We act surprised and shocked by it whenever it happens, even though death and corruption are everywhere we turn. Death is ridiculous because we weren't made for it—we weren't designed to die. The Bible tells us that, and our entire being yells that whenever we are at a funeral: "This is stupid! How could this happen?"

We weren't made to die; we were made to live forever.

We are made for the concert.

And the concert isn't the end of eternal life; it's the beginning.

It's the next phase of human existence.

My point is that as sure as there is a God who created you, loves you, and has called you not only to come to the concert but gave His Son to die so that you could have your ticket to the big show, there is also a devil who wants to sell you fake tickets your entire life. There is personified evil manipulating, distracting, and deceiving humanity. And this is all done through the work of idolatry.

As Alex explains in this book, Miami is full of fake tickets.

One could posit that it's one big Fake Ticket Master. It sells people all kinds of false senses of security—Money, Yachts, Success, Happiness, and more. It's all as fake and empty as the rentable Lamborghinis that people drive around the Beach.

Once again, there is nothing wrong with a Lambo. But if that's your ticket—if that's the measure of how well your life is going and what ultimately gives you the strongest sense of certainty that your life is going places—you've been played.

And this is the part where you should get a little angry and a bit indignant: someone is trying to pull the wool over your eyes constantly. You have a real enemy that hates you and wants you to buy into the proverbial scene so that you fill your life with empty distractions and vanities, never actually finding the real tickets.

The book you are holding is going to change all that. Alex has written this book to drive a truck through the mirage and set you up with the legit tickets. He's picking a fight with personified evil while hooking you up with a renewed vision of what life is meant to be.

Allow his story to reorient you.

Let this book capture your imagination and help you re-envision what the God who loves you is trying to show you.

What most of us need is a friend who destroys the fantasies that tend to grab our heads and hold us hostage to destructive thinking.

That's this book—this book is a bucket of cold water on the work of the devil.

Even us Christians need this. We need to be aware that we have a real enemy who is trying to capture our imagination through a competing vision of human flourishing. And we need continual reminders that the riches, cares, and concerns of this world are a massive hoax.

I love Miami. I love the culture, the food, the beach, the music, and the art. But I will use Miami; Miami won't use me. And I can get the best out of life when Jesus is my Lord and has my full attention. In fact, I can actually start enjoying the city the way I'm meant to when Jesus is at the center. Miami then becomes a better place—a more human place—when I'm in my right mind.

Jesus doesn't come to make life boring; He comes to make it better.

When I think of Alex, I think of someone who loves his city and loves life to the absolute max. And Jesus gave him that.

Allow Jesus to realign your priorities as you turn the pages of this book.

—Nathan Finochio.

PART 1:

HEAR THE WAR

SOUTH BEACH

CHAPTER ONE

"Welcome to Miami!"

Maybe you're like me—hearing that sentence instantly brings back memories. You know the song, the lyrics, the video. Sure, it might seem cheesy now, but back then, everyone was singing along and quoting the lines. This is the phrase almost everyone who grew up in the 90s remembers. The song, performed by Will Smith in 1997, became a global hit! The music video showcased Miami in all its glory. Will and his friends, frustrated by the freezing weather up north, leave a snow-covered Philadelphia and head to Miami. As soon as they land, the party begins! Will is cruising around Miami in a Bentley, soaking in everything the city has to offer—palm trees, clubs, beaches. I remember loving the song because Miami is my city, where I was born and raised. It was amazing to see my hometown on screen. *Welcome to Miami.*

Maybe when you think of Miami, you picture *Miami Vice*—the iconic outfits that dominated the airwaves, and the Ferrari Daytona speeding down Biscayne Boulevard along the water. Or perhaps you recall the famous "Catholics vs. Convicts" rivalry, when the Hurricanes, under Jimmy Johnson, were dominating college football in the '80s. Maybe it's the Cuban food, the nightclubs, or Pat Riley in his Armani suit running down the sideline, coaching the Heat.

Miami is a stunning city, lined with tall, beautiful palm trees stretching as far as the eye can see, and bathed in blazing sunshine almost year-round. Its nickname, "The Magic City," fits perfectly. Walking along the soft sands of the beach, feeling the grains sift between your toes as rhythmic waves crash against the shore, you can hear the sounds of Latin music, reggae, and hip-hop blending into a colorful cacophony that brings the streets alive with energy. The Art Deco buildings as the backdrop add to the charm. It's easy to see why I love my city!

The salty sea breeze is ever-present, carrying the scent of the ocean mixed with the tantalizing aroma of Cuban sandwiches being pressed, freshly fried plantains, and the strong, bittersweet fragrance of café cubano. You can almost taste the zing of lime squeezed onto fresh ceviche or the smoky sweetness of barbecue wafting through the air from a nearby party. It's a sensory overload—your skin tingles from the heat, your mouth waters from the flavors, and every inch of Miami makes you feel like you're in the middle of a celebration. I was born and raised here, and I genuinely believe it's the best city in the world. On any given day, you can head to the beach and find it full of people taking in the sun, enjoying the water, playing volleyball or football, or just having a great time. You can hear laughter, the music thumping from beach bars, and the buzz of conversations in countless languages. Miami is truly a melting pot. Some people might even be having *too* much fun—it's South Beach, after all. Wild, unpredictable, and incredible!

It's a vibrant city, filled with people from all corners of the world. The diversity of skin tones and cultures creates a full spectrum of color. It's a city that hums with life. You can taste the world in Miami—Cuban, Colombian, Nicaraguan, Peruvian, Jamaican, Haitian, and Mexican food, all within a few miles. A simple walk down the street becomes a journey through cultures, with the sounds of salsa, merengue, and Caribbean drums intertwining, while the vibrant colors of murals and street art dance in your peripheral vision.

And the Cuban coffee? You won't find anything like it anywhere else, and I'm convinced it's the best—though too much of it might be dangerous! The mix of cultures made my upbringing incredibly diverse, and I feel blessed to live where others vacation. From the famous Ocean Drive to Key Biscayne, Brickell, Wynwood, the Design District, Coconut Grove, and my hometown of Hialeah—just ask anyone about it.

Some of my favorite childhood memories are when my parents would gather us all into the car and take us on long drives through the city, often ending up at South Beach. Raised in a Hispanic Christian home, these moments were special. Seeing the city unfold before me—the very same one I often saw on TV or in movies—felt like an adventure. I loved going to the beach, seeing the brightly colored Lamborghinis and Rolls Royces cruising up and down Ocean Drive. All the cars had their music blasting, people were dancing, and everyone was heading to the water or to the most popular restaurants on the strip. On South

Beach, it seemed like life was amazing, and there was always a party.

Of course, growing up in a Christian household meant we would be listening to "Shout to the Lord," "Celebrate Jesus," or "Renuevame" (and if you know, you know—only Hispanic Christians would recognize that one) in the car just as loudly as the '69 Impala next to us was blasting Snoop and Dre. At those moments, my brother, sister, and I would sink into the backseat, peeking out of the windows, trying not to be noticed. And let's not forget the van—completely white, with huge black and orange stripes. The music was loud, but so was our van. It was so flashy that our friends nicknamed it the "Halloween" car. Good times.

Regardless of our choice of music or vehicle, I've always loved driving up and down the strip. Some of my best memories are from those drives. I remember one time, when I was older, we took a drive to South Beach during Super Bowl weekend. The streets were packed with celebrities, luxury cars, and the excitement building for the big game in my city. It was electric.

One night, though, things got out of hand. The avenue was swarming with cars and thousands of people everywhere. It felt like a parade gone wrong—cars honking, fights breaking out, music blaring, people screaming. I remember praying I'd make it out in one piece, and the moment I finished my prayer, I accelerated and crashed right into the car ahead of me on the packed Collins Ave. Best times!

South Beach truly is an amazing place. As a kid, we'd drive around and count the incredible cars, listening to their engines roar as they sped down Washington or Alton Road, past the palm trees and hotels. Just beyond the beach lies the world-famous Miami skyline, which so many have seen in movies and on TV.

To this day, I still love driving over the McArthur Causeway bridge. The view of Downtown Miami, with its skyscrapers rising over Biscayne Bay, is breathtaking. From that bridge, you can see massive cruise ships docked at the Port of Miami. If you drive by when they're sailing out, you'll catch passengers waving goodbye as they head off on vacation. You'll also spot the arena where the three-time NBA champions, and the best team in the NBA, the Miami Heat, play. If you didn't know, now you do! Just up the road is Star Island, home to enormous, luxurious mansions where famous celebrities live. As you can probably tell, I love Miami—the "Magic City" where I was born and raised.

Across the Bridge

As alluring as Miami is, there's more to it than the beaches, palm trees, and neon lights that everyone knows. When I got older and started venturing out with friends, I began to see a side of the city that no postcard or movie would ever show. Miami has layers—beneath the sunshine and luxury is a city weighed down by struggles that are often overlooked. I remember driving to Wynwood before it became the art district that tourists now flock to. Back then, it wasn't filled with murals or trendy restaurants. Instead, it was a neighborhood where people were caught in cycles of survival—chasing the next dollar or searching for their next high just to make it through another day.

My friend Kirk lived in Wynwood, and I would visit him often. He told me one day that developers had started offering money to families like his to relocate, making room for what was to come. He didn't know where they would go, but the change was coming. I witnessed things there that made me realize there was more to Miami than what I had seen from the backseat of the "Halloween" van with my parents. After dark, the streets took on a different vibe, and if you weren't familiar with the neighborhood, you had to stay on alert, always keeping an eye out for people who thought we were intruding on their hustle.

You could feel a sense of danger in the air, as if the city had shifted from the vibrant life of the beach to something rawer, darker.

I remember another friend taking us to a spot near downtown, notorious for being a place even the cops avoided due to gang violence. It made me wonder—why doesn't anyone talk about these places? What about the forgotten people I started to see in these neighborhoods—people just trying to survive? What about those being exploited, the women selling themselves on the streets of North Miami or Overtown as if their lives were worth nothing more than the next transaction? These are the parts of Miami no one shows—the neglected, the omitted.

When I was 12, my family moved to Cutler Ridge, on Miami's south side. It was there I learned about Naranja, Leisure City, Homestead, and Florida City. I began to see that Miami is more than the well-known South Beach that the world admires. Beyond the flashy cars, palm trees, and neon lights, there's a city that's broken—filled with pain, hurt, and confusion. It's not all sunshine and glamour like the movies, commercials, and postcards would have you believe. I love my city, and I still think it's the best in the world, but it's also a city shrouded in darkness.

Miami has a side rarely shown to the world. Across the bridge, there's pain, horrors, and evil. You cross that bridge, and suddenly you're in a place filled with poverty, drugs, and heinous crimes. This side of Miami is where, on some nights, you can feel the weight of despair in the air. It gets lost in the bright colors of music videos and the party scenes in movies, but like many cities, Miami has a very dark side.

I know it's obvious now—every city and town has its own struggles—but maybe we don't fully grasp just how dark it can be. That's what I began to see, and I felt burdened by this reality. More than the crime and violence, there was something deeper going on. When the sun set and night covered the city, it felt like a veil was lifted, revealing spiritual strongholds at play. Crack ruled the streets, prostitutes stood on every corner, and young lives were being destroyed before they ever had a chance to reach their destinies. Drugs flowed through the city, dark magic was visible on street corners, and you could see hunger and hopelessness etched into the faces of those wrecked by addiction.

The evil, the occult, and the destruction in Miami are so palpable you can almost smell it in the air. The Bible calls Satan the "prince of the power of the air" (Ephesians 2:2). Can we see that? Honestly, once you look behind the glitz of South Beach, the city isn't the paradise it's advertised to be. I came to this realization in my late teens. Miami, for all its beauty, is a war zone—a battleground where angels and demons clash in the night over human souls. It's a hot spot where the spirit of death prowls the streets, searching for lives to destroy. It's a war where lives are lost, and innocence is stolen in an instant. Young people overdose in the middle of the hottest nightspots, and no one seems to notice or care. Women are trafficked, young men are gunned down, and poison floods the veins of those trapped by addiction. This is Miami—the city of corruption and destruction. The magic of the city fades when you cross that bridge. This is Miami, the city God still loves.

War in the City

As I observed my city, I started to realize that there's a war happening right here, right in front of us. We hear about wars across the globe and see them on the news, but there's a battle raging in our own streets. I began to feel uneasy about the same South Beach I loved to drive through. I loved its vibrant colors and lively atmosphere, but I grew uncomfortable with the dark stories that unfolded every night—the lives exploited, the futures lost.

There's more to Miami than what meets the eye. There are far too many horror stories about what happens when the sun goes down and the lights dim. It's no paradise—it's a war zone. Sure, we all see the scenes of laughter, paparazzi snapping photos, and champagne spilling from oversized bottles with sparklers at Club Liv on Sunday nights. But beyond that, in the alleys, dark hallways, and bathrooms of these places lies another story. A recent study by the *Big City Health Inventory* reported that from 2010 to 2020, drug overdose deaths in cities nearly tripled, with the largest increase between 2019 and 2020. By 2020, at least 74% of overdose deaths involved opioids, up from 54% in 2010. That year, about 40 people a day died from overdoses in big cities.

Of course, this is nothing new. Big cities are often plagued by danger and drug wars. But what I'm addressing is something deeper—how we've conditioned ourselves to turn a blind eye just to keep the party going, to keep the money flowing, or simply to belong. I've heard too many stories of young people with bright futures losing their lives. I've sat in meetings with government agencies and heard reports of human trafficking happening in parts of my own city. The details are so heartbreaking and disturbing; they seem unreal. But it's all too real.

It hit me that what I celebrated and admired about my city was just a veneer, a glossy surface covering a reality few see—or choose to see. As we get older, we start to notice that it's not just happening in South Florida, but across the nation, across the world, in every city, town, and neighborhood. As amazing as some cities are with everything they offer, they also serve as a façade, distracting us while horrors unfold behind the scenes. I started to feel like I was just being entertained—numbed to the problems I didn't want to face. Then, I realized this distraction points to something even deeper. Just as the glitz and glamor of my city kept me from seeing the brokenness beneath, the world's allurements distract us from addressing the issues within our own souls. There is a war happening in the soul of every person.

This idea began to stir in my heart almost two decades ago: there's a war for our souls, waged by the things that seek to master them. Fame, money, and success may be obvious traps, but so are deeper struggles like trauma, dysfunction, hurt, bitterness, and resentment. These dangling carrots are designed to distract us from our potential, our destiny, and God's calling on our lives.

The great preacher Charles Spurgeon once said, "Consider how precious a soul must be when both God and the devil are after it." That's exactly it. Our soul—our mind, will, and emotions—encompasses our thoughts, desires, and feelings. It's so precious that opposing forces are constantly trying to capture our focus, to claim our time and attention. There's a war for our eyes and hearts, for our time and thoughts, for our habits and actions. Ultimately, there's a war for our worship. So, what will you and I worship? By worship, I mean what we think about, what we invest our time in, and what we live for. Will we chase after temporary things that leave us empty, or will we pursue the wholeness, healing, and life that God desires for us?

Yes, there's a war happening in our cities—that's obvious—but it goes much deeper than that. There's a war happening in every soul, including yours and mine. The war in our souls is what leads to the wars in our cities and the wars in our world. I'm convinced we've become so distracted, so enthralled by the world's exterior, that we neglect our interior world—our souls. How is your soul today? What consumes your thoughts, desires, feelings, and emotions?

Like my younger self, unaware of the darkness in my own city, how many of us walk around enjoying the magic of our surroundings, oblivious to the battle raging within our own souls? The Bible says in 1 Peter 5:8 (NIV), "Be alert and of sober mind.

Your enemy, the devil, prowls around like a roaring lion looking for someone to devour." We must be aware. We cannot continue living amused and distracted while our souls are ambushed, enslaved, and stifled by the lion.

Miami is a superficial city, obsessed with making everything look perfect on the outside. And yes, it's fine to look good on the outside, but that's not all there is. Some people kill themselves trying to maintain that exterior, even when their inside is filled with hurt, pain, resentment, confusion, bitterness, anger, and darkness. We can't continue living like this. Eventually, the battles within will spill over and affect the world around us. Just as a beautiful city can be destroyed by wars in the streets, so too can a beautiful life be destroyed by the wars raging within the soul.

I've witnessed so many beautiful lives that seemed perfect on the outside but were falling apart inside. Some had the looks others would kill for, the money, success, or fame, but as we talked and tried to help them, we realized the battles they faced ran far deeper than anyone could see.

Now, South Beach represents something greater to me. It looks amazing on the surface, but underneath lies brokenness. Don't get me wrong—South Beach is great, but it's also a mirage.

It symbolizes the success many people chase, but it's full of darkness and evil where so many get lost. It often makes me reflect and ask myself: how am I really doing? Am I too focused on my outward appearance and ignoring the state of my soul?

My perception of South Beach has drastically changed. For me, it represents humanity. It's like us—looking great on the outside, in pictures and videos, but possibly hiding pain, hurt, and inner turmoil. As I look at my city now, it forces me to examine my own soul and the war that rages within each of us. We can look good on the exterior, but still face a raging war on the interior. We need to be aware of the war happening around us, but more importantly, the one happening inside us. There's more than meets the eye. So, the next time you see South Beach on TV, with all its glitz and glamour, remember the war beneath the surface—because there *is* a war.

The Briefing Room

Step One - Awareness

Take one minute to reflect on your town, your city, and most importantly, your soul. Have you tried to evade or ignore issues, hurt, or perhaps pain in your world or soul? Is your soul at war?

Ask God to begin revealing what you may have hidden. Ask Him to open your eyes. This is the first step toward realizing there is a bigger plot taking place.

BORN FOR MORE

CHAPTER TWO

I was born on December 9, 1983, at Jackson Memorial Hospital in the heart of Miami. My parents had emigrated from Costa Rica a few years earlier, in their early twenties, in search of a better life and a brighter future. At the time, they were renting an apartment in Hialeah, where they lived with my older sister, Priscilla, who is two years my senior. A couple of years later, my younger brother, Manny, was born. We were a family of five, always together.

Every day, I thank God for my parents, and my appreciation for them grows with each passing year. I truly believe I have the best parents anyone could ask for—kind, loving, generous, God-fearing, honest, and incredibly hardworking. They instilled in me the values of hard work and faith in God.

My dad is the hardest-working man I've ever known. He's spent his life working, yet always managed to enjoy it. I still remember him coming home tired but always with a smile on his face. He's always been there for us, and he still is. My mother, beautiful and equally hardworking, has stood by his side every step of the way. She raised us, often relying solely on my dad's income to make ends meet.

That meant we grew up without cable TV, surviving on Pizza Rolls, LA Gears, and matching clothes from Kmart—but we made it through. My mom sacrificed a lot for us, and I'm eternally grateful. I had a great childhood—maybe not perfect, but pretty close. Not that there weren't any problems, but in my memory, those difficulties seem small compared to the grace God showed us.

I'm a church kid, through and through. We were raised in church, involved in everything—Royal Rangers, DC Talk, T-Bone, you name it (and if you know, you know!). Pray for me. Growing up in church meant participating in every activity available, and even some they probably invented. We had Sunday School Bible verse competitions, played every barnyard character in Christmas plays, wore suits and ties for Easter, and turned off the lights at home for Halloween because we had "Holy Night" at church! One Holy Night, I even played the referee in a David vs. Goliath boxing match. True story.

One thing my parents did that always stood out was baby dedications. They followed the Christian tradition of dedicating us as babies before God and our church community. It's a beautiful custom still practiced in many Christian churches today.

A group of parents, with their newborns, stand before the congregation to dedicate their child to God. It's deeply profound and meaningful. Jesus Himself was dedicated as a baby, so we continue to follow that tradition. I think it's special—a commitment before God and family to raise the child in a God-centered environment, with the help of the community, because, as the saying goes, it takes a village to raise a child.

My parents told me that when they dedicated me at a small church in Hialeah, the pastor holding me said I was a big baby (I'm still not sure if that was a compliment or not) and that I looked like I was going to be a boxer. Years later, when they shared that story with me, I loved it! Besides the "big baby" part, I don't think the pastor had any idea how meaningful those words would become to me later in life.

As I grew up and witnessed the darkness in my city and the destruction in my friends' lives, I felt a call to action. I couldn't sit still and turn a blind eye. As I watched the war in my soul and the souls of those around me—souls captivated and deceived by lies—I knew it was time for fighters to rise and speak up.

Over time, those words spoken by the pastor began to inspire me. I've become a fighter, but not in the literal sense. I'm a boxer in the battle against the darkness and lies that fill my city—and the same lies that fill so many of our souls. And those words weren't just meant for me. We are all called to fight the serpent that tempted us in Eden. We must stand against the lies that try to keep us from becoming the image of God we were meant to be.

As our souls process the world around us, we each face a decision. Do we allow ourselves to be mastered by these things, or do we stand in faith and believe we were created for something more? You were designed with purpose, talents, gifts, and skills that are uniquely yours to offer the world. You can experience freedom, peace, joy, and hope. Recognize the war, and decide today—a fighter is born.

Refuse to lay down and let life pass you by without ever fully realizing all that God has for you. You can fight back against the currents of life and the spiritual powers that want you and me to become apathetic and average. Psalm 144:1-2 says, "Blessed be the LORD, my rock, who trains my hands for war, and my fingers for battle." God is for you and helps you achieve the greater purpose He has for your life!

Church Kids

Growing up, my parents were youth pastors at a small church in Hialeah, and they helped out wherever they could. This meant we were in church every day. I remember all the events—the plays, movie nights, and more. Even after they were no longer youth pastors, they remained deeply involved. My mom worked at the church, and my dad helped out whenever he could. We literally grew up in the church. Every summer, we spent our days walking through the church offices, playing on the playground, and roaming the halls. So, while we didn't have a Nintendo, we did have *McGee and Me* videotapes—a Christian show about a kid with a cartoon friend—and Carman CDs, featuring a super energetic Christian artist who turned gospel music into a full production show. We might not have had the latest gaming console, but our church experience was packed with its own kind of fun!

As I got older, I started helping out in church. Despite the things we look back on and laugh about now, it was a special time. I helped everywhere! I volunteered with the kids' teams and Sunday School, where they had me teach and lead the sports department—despite having no clue what I was doing. I also assisted on the sound team for a bit, worked with the host team, security, and more. I even got involved with teams like **EEE (Extreme Evangelism Explosion)** for years, where we'd drive all over the city on Tuesday nights, witnessing and telling people about God—those nights were wild! I led youth prayer, helped with the video team, and spent summers at Vacation Bible School showing *Veggie Tales* movies to students. I've truly seen it all!

I'm so grateful to have grown up in the church. Psalm 84:10 says, *"Better is one day in His courts than a thousand elsewhere."* I could complain about the odd things we had to endure, but looking back, it was the best thing for me. Beyond the silliness we laugh at now, I learned so much—responsibility, leadership, organization, and administration, to name a few.

Let me take a moment to speak to those who, like me, were raised in the church. Yes, we had an interesting upbringing—sometimes embarrassed by certain things, but blessed by it all. However, we need to be careful not to become so familiar with church life that we start to take it lightly.

Many of us who grew up in church can reach a point where everything becomes routine. Another service becomes just another service. We like it, sure, but we start detaching ourselves from the deeper meaning of it all—the profoundness and beauty of the body being built, the gifts at work, and the lives at stake. We risk becoming indifferent. We let the silly things we mock block our view of the powerful work God is doing.

We think we've seen it all, heard it all. We know the songs, the routines, and the people by name. We know when to stand and sit, how to act, and we have all the Christian phrases down—"Amen, brother," "Blessed and highly favored," "So good." But please don't let church become a routine! Don't let the things of God become so familiar that they no longer move you. Don't become indifferent or passive.

Now, a word to those who weren't raised in church. Maybe you've just started your relationship with God or recently began attending a local church. You've probably started noticing the little things that can distract us from God's vision and plans. We begin magnifying small problems and letting them affect our hearts. We allow broken people to break our zeal.

Get Your Gloves

This is where I found myself at times. I knew God. I knew His Word, how to pray, and how to do church. I was well-versed in "Christian life," like so many of us who grew up in church. I wasn't getting involved in the wrong things; I listened to *Newsboys*, *Cross Movement*, and *Michael W. Smith*. I knew right from wrong.

But if I'm honest, there were times when I found myself sitting in the back of the church auditorium, just talking with friends, not paying attention, and waiting to leave. I was indifferent. My heart was cold, apathetic to the things happening around me and within me. I wasn't aware. I would help out because that's what we all did, but I didn't grasp the bigger picture. I was clueless.

As time went on, I knew something wasn't right. There had to be more—more than just attending Sunday services, hearing a message, and hanging out. More than being on the sound team or helping without hearing God's voice for my own life. I knew there was more. I was made for more than this. There had to be more than being a youth leader and hanging out at summer camps. More than Friday nights laughing and ending up at IHOP (the restaurant, not the church) until 3 a.m.

Don't get me wrong—those things were great, and many of them shaped who I am today. But too often, I was just there, taking up space. I wasn't in tune with God's Spirit. I began to ask myself: Am I really here to encounter God, or am I just waiting for the service to end so I can meet my friends?

If you find yourself stuck in this routine now, I'm pleading with you—stop, think, and realize there is more to church than the four walls! There's more to youth night than a small message and some fun! There's more to church than just showing up occasionally. God wants to do so much more with you! I pray that, just as I was convicted, you are awakened by the Holy Spirit. I pray that a deeper revelation enters your spirit and opens your eyes. God has bigger plans! He loves you and has gifted you to be His ambassador, no matter your age, past, or present. God wants to use you!

When I was about 17, I began to realize that God wanted more from me than just attendance. He didn't want me sitting in the back, wasting time while my city—Miami, the city I love—was being torn apart in the dark. I knew something was wrong. Slowly, I became aware. I started to get bolder in my faith. I wanted to know more of God, to learn, and to find out what He had for me, my friends, and my city. I wanted to know God like never before. That's when I became aware of the war.

I ask you today—what are you doing with what God has given you? How are your city and friends? I pray you recognize the opportunity in front of you to make a difference. Don't squander your days and strength. Don't take anything for granted. Don't fall for the distractions of this world. Realize where you've been caught in the snare.

There's a powerful story in 1 Samuel 17 that most of us know by heart. Goliath, the giant, is threatening and taunting the Israelites, poised to obliterate them. No one dares to challenge him. And of course, we all know who finally steps up—David. We know this story well. But here's the part that always stands out to me: the Bible says in 1 Samuel 17:16, *"For forty days the Philistine came forward and took his stand, morning and evening."*

This wasn't just one day of intimidation. Goliath came out *every day for 40 days*! Yet, no one did anything. Nothing. Not a single person made a move—until David showed up. We know how the story ends, but think about this: for 40 days, the people endured threats, abuse, and oppression, and no one took a stand. That's how I feel about what's happening in our world today. It's been days, weeks, even months, with the enemy hurling war-like words at our souls. And very few are standing up to fight back. It's time.

Perhaps you didn't grow up in church and haven't been to one in a long time. Maybe your upbringing was different from mine, but you too have been sensing and feeling that there is more for your life. Like many friends I've met, maybe you've let the past, mistakes, and trauma hold you back and weigh you down. You've let time slip by without fully living up to your potential and becoming the best version of yourself. Your time and energy have been spent on things that don't offer a fulfilling return.

You are a fighter, too. You need to believe that. You were born to fight. There is a war for the human soul. Will our generation continue to sit back, mesmerized and hypnotized by everything this culture offers? Are we going to spend all our days and energy chasing things that satisfy only for a moment?

Jesus asked, *"What will it profit a man if he gains the whole world, yet forfeits his soul? Or what can a man give in exchange for his soul?"* (Matthew 16:26). So yes, enjoy life, I certainly do, but we must also stay focused and fight. Guard your soul, and fight by choosing better, eternal options.

It's time to take a stand. There's more to your life than just working for a paycheck, taking vacations, or curating the perfect Instagram post. There's more than attending a church service and seeing no real change in our cities or our lives. There's more than just getting by and living this life as if there's not more at stake. As we begin this journey together through this book, my prayer is that you would pick up the gloves for your soul.

You don't have to spend the rest of your life letting people, places, or things decide who you are, what you wear, what you do, or who you worship. We can reclaim control over our lives. You and I can live in freedom, peace, fullness, and prosperity.

You don't have to be subjected to disorder, dysfunction, and confusion. As believers in Jesus Christ, we can walk through this war with a peace that surpasses all understanding—not just surviving, but thriving. And there's an opportunity for you to help others in the midst of this war as well.

Fight today. Fight for your family, your city, and your future!

The Briefing Room

Step Two - Adjust

Take one minute to write down the things you've perhaps allowed to linger for too long. Maybe it's harmful self-talk, faithlessness, or self-sabotage. Write down what has made you become complacent with all that God is doing and wants to do, and ask the Spirit of God to reveal it. He will.

NO SLEEP TILL…

CHAPTER THREE

My high school experience was amazing. I don't know how it was for you, but I had a blast. I went to Miami Southridge High School—hands down, the best school in the city. Ask anyone. When I think back, I have so many great memories of those years. I went to school with a lot of friends from my church, along with other friends from the neighborhood, so we all grew up together. I remember the pep rallies, TV production classes, and driving out for lunch. Back in the early 2000s, we were still allowed to leave campus for lunch, and we'd head to Wendy's or Burger King and have the best time. Sure, our grades may not have been top-notch, but the memories definitely were.

If there was ever a perfect place to sleep, it was on a desk in a high school classroom. I remember one day, a friend of ours was fighting sleep so hard. Have you ever seen someone do the head nod when they're trying not to fall asleep? That was him that day.

He was going down hard, repeatedly jolting awake and sitting up straight. It looked like he was about to snap his neck with all the head-bobbing. I'll never forget—at one point, he was nearly out for the count when he suddenly woke up, snapped his head back, and started acting like he was just nodding to some music. He tried to play it off, like we didn't just see him struggling. *Really, bro?* The entire class had been watching him for a solid 10 minutes, trying not to laugh. Falling asleep in the wrong place is embarrassing, and trust me, I've seen it happen more than a few times. It's always funny—and almost never good.

One time, we were at an all-night prayer meeting at church—a "vigilia," as it's called in Spanish churches. I was about 11 or 12 years old, and a few of us kids were sneaking in and out of the service while the adults prayed. At one point, they called people to the front to pray near the altar, and my dad was one of them. He knelt on the floor, resting his head on the stage, deep in prayer.

As time passed, everyone else finished praying and returned to their seats, but not my dad. I remember thinking, *What a prayer warrior! He's unstoppable!* He was still there, praying passionately, while the rest of the congregation watched in admiration. Then, after what felt like an eternity, he suddenly jolted awake and looked around, confused. Turns out, he wasn't deep in prayer—he had fallen asleep right there in front of everyone!

These stories are funny, and I'm sure you've experienced something similar. But when I reflect on our cities and souls, I see a deeper parallel. As I became aware of the battles happening in our streets and within ourselves, I realized the same thing happens to us spiritually. Falling asleep—physically, spiritually, mentally, or emotionally—in the wrong place and time is far too common.

We can be physically awake yet spiritually asleep. It's like sleepwalking through life. My wife, Diana, and I once lived with my sister for a few months when we first got married, and I remember being woken up by my nephew sleepwalking. He'd knock on the door or just wander down the hallway, eyes closed but walking. It was creepy, to be honest, and it reminded me of how many of us live. We're awake and going through the motions—work, school, church, friendships, life in general—but we're asleep to God's purposes, plans, and gifts.

The concept of "spiritual sleepwalking" sets up a powerful metaphor for how many of us go through life on autopilot, unaware of the deeper purpose God has for us. To bring this home, expanding on the signs and indicators of spiritual sleepwalking can help people identify it in themselves. For example, spiritual sleepwalking might look like going through the motions—attending church, saying the right things, and keeping busy with life, but lacking a real connection with God's purpose. You're physically present, but your heart isn't engaged. You pray, but it feels mechanical, or you read the Bible, but the words don't stir you anymore.

People who are spiritually asleep often feel like they're stuck in a cycle—they might experience dissatisfaction, numbness, or a sense of aimlessness, despite outwardly having everything together. It's easy to miss the warning signs because everything seems fine from the outside. They aren't blatantly rebellious or "off track," but their soul isn't actively engaged in the fight for what truly matters.

It's like sleepwalking—just as someone might get up, walk around, and even interact without being fully aware of their surroundings, many of us go through life without being fully conscious of God's presence. We're busy, productive, and on the surface, everything seems normal, but spiritually, we're disconnected, drifting, or ignoring that inner nudge that says, "There's more."

Now is the time to wake up! Being spiritually awake means being in tune with God, alert to the opportunities to serve, love, and grow. It's about being intentional—seeing beyond the daily routine and realizing that God is calling you to something greater. It means recognizing the fight for your soul and actively participating in it, not letting the world's noise lull you into a state of passivity.

If this resonates with you—if you feel like you're sleepwalking through your relationship with God, going through the motions without a deeper connection—it's time to stop and ask Him to wake you up. Don't let the comfort of routine dull your spiritual senses. Now is the moment to rise and engage in the life God has for you, fully awake, fully aware, and ready for the battle ahead. If there was ever a time to be careful not to fall asleep, it's now. This is not the time to be asleep spiritually!

Window Seat

There's a story in the Bible that I love—it's found in Acts 20. It's fascinating. The Apostle Paul, who had been traveling, preaching, teaching, and helping start churches, was spending one final night in Troas. This night was special. He was surrounded by people gathered in a third-floor room, eager to hear him preach because he would leave the next day, likely never to return. Paul was a living legend, and everyone wanted to hear him speak one last time.

In the room that night was a young man named Eutychus. It was a historic moment, and Eutychus chose to sit by the open window. I get it—window seats are the best. But after some time, Paul, who had a lot to say, was still preaching, and Eutychus began to get really tired. Has that ever happened to you in church? It happens all the time. Like my friend from high school and like my dad, Eutychus fought sleep, but eventually, he gave in.

He was overcome by sleep and fell out of the window from the third floor. What?! Imagine being in that church service—Eutychus fell out and died! Crazy, right?

Everyone rushed downstairs and found Eutychus lying there, lifeless. This beautiful, historic night had taken a tragic turn. I can imagine the gasps, the panic, people screaming. Were his parents there? His siblings? It must have been chaos. The story tells us that Paul came down, calmed everyone, and reassured them that Eutychus was still alive. Miraculously, Eutychus came back to life. Paul simply went back upstairs and continued teaching like nothing had happened. And afterward, they all enjoyed a meal together! It's wild—Eutychus had fallen from a third story, been dead for minutes, and yet he was perfectly fine afterward.

This is one of the wildest stories of a church service in the Bible! As I've read it, I've often wondered about Eutychus. Why did he choose to sit by the window? Was he disengaged? Was he daydreaming, distracted? How could someone be sitting in front of a living legend like Paul and yet fall asleep?

Of course, there could be many reasons why Eutychus fell asleep—maybe he'd had a long day, or maybe the room was just too warm—but I can't help but think there's more to the story. Maybe Eutychus was in the room, but not really *in* the room.

Maybe his body was present, but his mind was elsewhere. This makes me think: what if this story is a picture of us?

Let's consider a broader application here, but I think it fits. What if Eutychus represents the tension between **religion** and **relationship**? He was in the middle of something incredibly important—a gathering led by Paul—but he wasn't tuned in. It reminds me of how we can be physically present in worship but not spiritually engaged. We might be really good at the rituals but poor at the relationship. Some of us have been religious for a long time. We go to church, sing the songs, know the verses, but aren't connected in our hearts. We're not leaning in or fully alive to what God is doing. I truly believe God doesn't just want our physical presence—He wants our spiritual worship.

What if we are like Eutychus right now? Sitting by a window, gazing out into the world, distracted, while our souls are being rocked to sleep. It was the great Leonard Ravenhill who once wrote, "At this grim hour, the world sleeps in the darkness - and the church sleeps in the light."

Own, Don't Rent

This reminds me of a story from when I was about 12. One of our church friends had his car in the shop, and in the meantime, they gave him a rental—a convertible Ford Mustang. It was a beautiful car! One Sunday after church, he offered to take us all for a spin, and we were thrilled. We drove around Hialeah, loving every second of it. A few days later, I asked my friend about the car, and he said his dad had returned it because it was just a rental. We had enjoyed the ride, but it wasn't ours. We didn't own it.

That's how I think many of us treat our relationship with God—we're renting, not owning. We give Him our attention on Sundays, but we return to our regular lives on Monday. We've rented our hearts instead of giving God ownership of our lives. But God doesn't want to rent—He wants to own. He desires our entire heart, mind, body, and soul. He doesn't just want church attendance; He wants real, heartfelt worship. He doesn't just want our bodies in church—He wants our hearts in worship.

This is what the spiritual war is all about. We were created in the image and likeness of God, and our hearts are wired for worship. The question is, who or what are we worshiping? We live in a world that is deeply religious, whether we realize it or not. Just look at how we treat celebrities, athletes, and entertainers. We worship them. People will faint when they meet their favorite star or throw themselves at their feet—that's worship.

We all have different views on the spirituality of our culture, but I believe we are incredibly religious. Most people worldwide engage in some form of tradition or activity that reflects a spiritual longing—whether that's attending church, using prayer beads, or holding onto objects that represent something higher.

While some of these practices aren't necessarily bad, they should never replace a relationship with the Creator. A real relationship is alive and vibrant; it involves communication, affection, and sacrifice. God desires more than just religious rituals or church attendance. He longs for a deep, thriving relationship. That means talking to Him, hearing from Him, and giving Him our full attention every day, just as we would in any meaningful relationship with someone we love.

Otherwise, we risk going through the motions—engaging in spiritual activities without true spiritual vitality. We can *do* spiritual things without *being* spiritual beings. We need to examine our lives and ask ourselves: Are we truly present with our whole being? Are we alive—mind, body, and soul—to God and all that He has for us? God doesn't want half of us; He wants all of us. He loves you more than you can imagine and desires a real relationship with you. Give Him your whole heart daily, and watch that relationship flourish, bringing blessings you never thought possible.

After reevaluating, many of us might be surprised to discover that what we've had is **religion**, not **relationship**. Jesus said in Matthew 7:21, *"Not everyone who says to me, 'Lord, Lord,' will enter the kingdom of heaven, but only the one who does the will of my Father who is in heaven."* When I think of Eutychus, I consider his position and posture. He was sitting at a window, likely comfortable enough to doze off on a historic night. Position and posture matter. Where are we sitting in life? Do we have a posture that shows interest in God and what He is doing? Are we awake to His plans for us?

Windows of Life

The windows of life are everywhere, and they can easily distract us from what's happening right in front of us. We look out through these windows—whether they're social media, TV, or even the world around us—focusing on what others are doing, what's trending, and what's in or out. We become so caught up in watching people, restaurants, lounges, fashion, and pop culture that we miss the present moment. I believe many of us are consumed by these windows in life, so distracted that we miss what God is doing right now.

You see it happening all around us today. Social media is one of the biggest windows through which we get distracted. Walk into any restaurant, and you'll often find entire families sitting together, yet no one is talking because everyone is glued to their phones or tablets. It even happens while driving—people trying to scroll through Instagram, Facebook, Twitter, or TikTok while navigating traffic. If we're honest, we've all probably done it ourselves—recording videos while walking, even while driving! This is our world now. We are so invested in pop culture—who's dating whom, what's trending, what's gone viral—that we lose sight of what God is doing right in front of us. We are physically awake but spiritually asleep.

According to Belle Wong, J.D., of Forbes, "In 2023, an estimated 4.9 billion people use social media worldwide. This number is expected to jump to approximately 5.85 billion users by 2027. It's absolutely wild how many of us live on our phones." Forbes also reported that "the average person spends about 145 minutes on social media every day," and "to put this into perspective, if the average person maintained this usage over a lifespan of 73 years, the end result is an astonishing 5.7 years spent on social media platforms!" They also found that 39% of U.S. social media users admitted to feeling "the addictive pull of the digital rabbit hole," with 9% of these users agreeing completely with the statement, "I am addicted to social media."

These kinds of statistics provide a glimpse into a society that is entertained and asleep. We are all prone to fall asleep spiritually and miss out on what God has for us. There's another powerful story in the Bible where Jesus takes three of His closest disciples to the Mount of Olives to pray in the Garden of Gethsemane. The name "Gethsemane" in Hebrew means "a place to press for oil." There were giant stone slabs used to press olives, extracting oil from them. It's a symbolic picture of the suffering and pressure Jesus was about to endure. In that garden, the greatest spiritual battle for the souls of mankind was being fought as Jesus prepared to drink the cup of death for our sins.

You would think that in such a moment, His best friends—Peter, James, and John—would be there for Him, offering care and comfort. But the Bible tells us otherwise. All three of them fell asleep. Three times, Jesus came back to check on them, and each time they were snoring, completely unaware of the gravity of what was happening.

If Peter, James, and John—heroes of the faith—could fall asleep, so can we. In Matthew 26:40-41, after finding them asleep again, Jesus says something profound: *"Couldn't you men keep watch with me for one hour? Watch and pray so that you will not fall into temptation. The spirit is willing, but the flesh is weak."*

Jesus confronts them. He tells them to stay awake, to be watchful and prayerful. He warns them that while the spirit is willing, the flesh is weak, and that prayer is essential to avoid temptation. If we stay alert and prayerful, it will be far more beneficial than gazing out of life's windows, distracted. It's time to wake up!

If we want to have a vibrant spiritual life and receive everything God has for us, we must stay awake! In the 1800s, the great preacher Charles Spurgeon said, *"Satan seeks to lull God's prophets into slumber, for he knows that dumb dogs that are given to sleep will never do any very great injury to his cause. He must think it almost as well to have a Christian asleep as to have him dead: he would certainly sooner see him in hell, but next to that, he is most glad to see him rocked in the cradle of presumption, fast asleep."*

I love how the story of Eutychus ends in the book of Acts. After he fell from the window and died, Paul prayed for him, and he came back to life. How amazing is that? I also love that Luke, the author of Acts, includes the detail of his name—Eutychus—when he didn't have to. He could've just said, "some young man fell out of a window and was revived," but he didn't. Eutychus' name means "Fortunate" or "Lucky."

He was certainly fortunate that Paul was there, but more than that, he was fortunate that the same Holy Spirit who raised Jesus from the dead was in the room that night!

That same Holy Spirit is alive today, and all you have to do is ask Him to revive you! Have you fallen asleep spiritually? Have weeks, months, or maybe even years gone by without you truly engaging in your relationship with God? Don't sleep on this! God has so much more for you! He loves you, He's for you, and He's on your side! Wake up to the wonder, the blessings, the plans, and the purposes He has for you! It's not too late—you're not too far gone!

The other day, I was working on my laptop, and a notification popped up: *"This MacBook will soon sleep unless connected to a power source."* Those words jumped out at me! The power of connection is vital.

Stay connected to God and all He has for you! As Paul writes in Ephesians 5:14, *"Wake up, sleeper, rise from the dead, and Christ will shine on you!"* I love those words. Wake up! Let the light of Christ shine on you. Today, ask the Holy Spirit to revive you—and He will!

The Briefing Room

Step Three - Awaken

Take one minute to analyze which areas of your life you have left unchecked. Have they caused you to sleepwalk through life lately? Are you feeling disorganized or undisciplined? You are alive but sleeping, functioning but on automatic. Ask God to awaken you to all He has for you—His plans, dreams, and purposes today!

LET IT RAIN

CHAPTER FOUR

Have you ever thought about your eye and how incredible it is? The human eye—it's absolutely amazing! It's a true work of art. The variety of colors, its structure, and its function are all so complex and unique. No human-made camera can come close to matching it. The eye captures an incredible amount of information, processing it through its vessels, nerves, and components.

The eye's extraordinary capabilities work seamlessly with the human mind—another mind-blowing creation of God. The eye and brain are perfectly synchronized. What the eye captures, the brain immediately processes, meditates on, and deciphers within milliseconds. Think about it: as you're reading these words, your brain is taking in everything your eyes see and almost instantly interpreting it. That's wild! These two creations are nothing short of miraculous. And because the eye and brain work together, we can say this: what you focus your eye on, you set your mind on.

Some might say the mind has an "eye" of its own. The brain can visualize, imagine, and create images and thoughts without even needing to physically see something. It has the remarkable ability to generate dreams, ideas, and visions. Scientific research shows that both the eye and the brain provide us with constant information throughout the day, whether externally through sight or internally through imagination. We are always thinking—our minds are always processing.

This incredible connection between sight and thought should make us pause and reflect. The fact that we can both see and imagine means that whatever we look at or visualize can consume our thoughts, and those thoughts ultimately shape who we become. Simply put: **we are what we think about.** We become what we focus on most, whether it's through our natural eyes or our mind's eye.

Human Becomings

We are not only human *beings*, but we are also human *becomings*. This term, which I've come to love over the past few years, reflects the idea that we are constantly evolving, hopefully growing into something stronger, wiser, and more mature. As *becomings*, what we focus on influences who or what we become. The more we think about something, the more it shapes our actions, choices, and desires. What we visualize affects our decisions, what we pursue, and how we live.

The marketing and advertising industry has mastered this concept. It's a billion-dollar industry that knows how to influence human *becomings*. They understand that a well-crafted advertisement can make us desire the product they're selling because we're all trying to improve—become more successful, get ahead, and learn new things. The amount of money spent to capture our attention is mind-blowing. Just think: companies spend millions of dollars for a mere 30-second commercial during the Super Bowl because they know how powerful visuals are. Some of us can even recall the most memorable commercials from years ago because our eyes and brains captured them so vividly.

These companies know that over 100 million people are watching, and a visual that catches the eye or a catchy song can make their brand unforgettable. Every day, marketing teams gather in conference rooms, brainstorming how to capture our attention because if they can grab our gaze, they can capture our hearts.

If what we see and think about plays such a crucial role in shaping us, we need to pay close attention to what we focus on. And that's easier said than done, especially with the constant distractions in life. My ADHD doesn't help—one minute I'm browsing 15 tabs, texting five people, and listening to music, and the next I've forgotten to respond to half of those texts. New things constantly capture our eyes and minds.

I've noticed the same thing happens with my faith. I can have my eyes and thoughts focused on God's promises, His Word, and His plans for me, but the moment something else grabs my attention, I'm distracted. Anybody else?

One minute, I'm feeling great, focused on God's truth, and the next I'm scrolling through social media. Suddenly, I feel like I'm not doing enough, not good enough—like I'm inadequate. I start questioning if I'm qualified, smart, or creative enough, and just like that, I'm discouraged. All of this happens in less than five minutes! It affects my being and becoming because what I focus on starts to influence what I think about.

I want to challenge you, if I may. Take an audit of your affections. What have your eyes been focused on lately? Or better yet, what have you been thinking about the most? Where have your affections been? Do you have too many things weighing on your heart and mind at once? It's time to examine what we've been focusing on. The more we gaze at something, the more time and value we assign to it. And when we give something time and value, in a way, we're worshiping it.

Before you think that sounds crazy, let me explain.

I know it may sound strange or even bizarre to say we worship Instagram reels, Twitter feeds, the stock market, or cable news, but hear me out. The concept of worship is deep and profound—it could easily fill an entire book to explain what biblical worship truly means. Worship is more than just singing songs. To simplify, one aspect of worship involves giving our time, mind, and soul to something we consider worthy. It's about elevating something or someone above everything else in how we view and think about it.

With that understanding, we can see that if what I spend most of my time on affects how I walk, think, and process life—if it shapes my becoming—I may be worshiping it. As human *beings*, what we dedicate our time to plays a massive role in who and what we will become in the years ahead. We will inevitably become what we worship. So the key question is: ***Who or what do we worship?***

The more we spread our worship across multiple things, the more divided our hearts become. In a world filled with advertising, marketing giants, and social media platforms all vying for our attention, it's safe to say we're in the middle of a war—a war for our souls.

If nothing else has captured your attention in this book, please focus on this: There is a war for your soul. This war is for your mind, will, emotions, and ultimately, your heart. Everything and everyone wants your attention, your money, your time, and your heart. The more you give to things of lesser value, the more fragmented and divided you become. So with that information, we can say, to win the war of your soul, you have to win the battle for your sight.

I've spent the past few years reflecting on how we've invested too much of our thoughts, time, money, affections, and emotions into things that aren't truly worth it. Our culture feels too cluttered; our society seems overly saturated with distractions that are robbing our attention, leaving us empty, broken, and divided. These distractions are sapping the fire out of our lives. In your journey of becoming, do not give your worship to something that's not worthy of it.

Divided Souls

There's a perfect example of this division in the Bible. In 1 Kings 18, we see how divided worship can lead to brokenness. During this time, Israel had been split into two kingdoms: the northern kingdom of Israel and the southern kingdom of Judah. In Chapter 18, we meet King Ahab, a king who worshipped false gods and was entirely wicked. God sent the prophet Elijah to warn and judge him with a drought.

The people of Israel had taken their eyes off the one true God. They began to worship new gods, mixing their faith with the surrounding cultures. Even though God had delivered their ancestors from Egypt, they began worshipping Baal, a false god, and engaging in ungodly practices. They wanted to worship God while also worshipping Baal. They were divided in their allegiance.

In 1 Kings 17, Elijah declared a three-year drought in the land. The drought was intended to prove that Baal, the so-called god of rain and fertility, was powerless before the true living God.

Despite three years of drought, the people of Israel were so captivated by the world around them that they couldn't see that Baal was powerless to end their suffering.

In 1 Kings 18:21, Elijah confronts the people, saying, *"How long will you falter between two opinions? If the Lord is God, follow Him; but if Baal, follow him."* But the people said nothing. They were torn, divided between two allegiances. The word "falter" here means "to skip or hop back and forth." They were undecided, stuck between two opinions. This is important because indecision leads to ineffectiveness.

In failing to make a decision for God, they had, in essence, made a decision against Him. The problem with indecision is that it often causes people to do nothing. There will be moments in life when we must make decisions about what will capture our attention, heart, time, and worship. Whatever is not worthy, healthy, or good must be cut out, lest it drags us down into the mire. Billy Graham once said, *"There is no room in the throne of your heart for two gods."* You cannot have a divided soul.

It's been said that someone once asked Alexander the Great how he conquered the world, and his reply was, *"By not wavering."* He didn't allow indecision to stop him. In James 1:6-8, we are told, *"But let him ask in faith, with no doubting, for he who doubts is like a wave of the sea driven and tossed by the wind. For let not that man suppose that he will receive anything from the Lord; he is a double-minded man, unstable in all his ways."* When we are divided or indecisive, we fail to accomplish what we're meant to be.

To summarize the rest of the story from 1 Kings, Elijah calls out the people who were serving Baal and challenges them to a showdown on Mount Carmel. Both sides would set up an altar with a sacrifice, and whichever God sent down fire would be the true God.

The prophets of Baal went first. They prayed, shouted, danced, and even cut themselves, trying to get Baal's attention, but nothing happened. No fire. No answer. Nothing.

The prophet Elijah had had enough. He called the people to him, set up his altar, and even drenched it with water. Then he called on God, and immediately, fire came down from heaven, consuming Elijah's entire sacrifice! Real fire from heaven torched everything! What a scene that must have been—an unforgettable moment.

This battle took place on Mount Carmel many years ago, but in a very similar way, there is a battle happening today in the hearts of all of us. We may find ourselves gazing at or even worshipping false gods of validation, titles, recognition, lust, comparison, greed, or envy. We live in a society where it's incredibly easy to pick up these false gods that constantly call for our attention. Our world pressures us to live a life of compromise, leaving our souls divided, without us realizing that a war is being waged.

The fire is missing. Throughout history, fire has represented light, life, and power. We've heard expressions like "fire in their eyes" or "fire in their soul," symbolizing passion and vitality. I believe millions of people around the world have placed their eyes, minds, or souls on the wrong things. They've allowed their attention or worship to be drawn to objects that cannot give the satisfaction, life, or fire they promise.

The fire of life is missing in the hearts of humanity. The material things we chase—cars, houses, relationships, one-night stands, vacations, positions—are not fulfilling us. They don't provide the fire we need to live a full, satisfied life. Instead, we're left feeling empty, depleted, and lacking.

I truly believe we're in a time where we must examine our souls. By "soul," I mean our hearts, will, and emotions. We need to stop and inspect what's taking up residence in our souls.

What's occupying our time and attention? It's healthy to reflect on what we've given our eyes, minds, and hearts to.

There's a war—a war for your worship. What have you and I been worshipping? When we worship things more than God, those things become gods to us. When we prioritize people, places, and things over God, it leads us down an unhealthy path. It doesn't have to be something dark or evil—it can even be something good. But what I've learned is that when a good thing becomes a *god* thing, it turns into a bad thing. It no longer provides the fire we need to truly live.

There's a war—a war in our hearts, in our culture, and in our society. There's a war for our attention, our souls. It goes even further—there's a war for our relationships, our marriages, our families, our children, our values, and our morals. When our eyes are fixed on the wrong things, the fire can go missing in all these areas. How's the fire in your soul?

This war isn't happening in a world we can see with our natural eyes, but it's a real fight for our worship, our attention, and our allegiance. What's occupying the view of your eyes, the thoughts of your mind, and the seat of your heart? Who or what are you worshipping? If there's a fire missing in your life, it's likely because a battle is being fought for your heart.

God wants more than just for you to survive—He wants you to thrive. He desires for you to live with a fire in your heart, soul, and entire being. He wants your relationships, your marriage, your dreams, your potential, and your aspirations to be filled with passion and purpose. Today, decide in your heart to serve God with everything you have, and your soul will find the fire it needs.

The Briefing Room

Step Four - Aim

Take one minute to reflect on your eyes and mind. Have you let them wander and wonder for too long on worthless things? Start redirecting your heart little by little to the right place. Aim at God and the things above. Focus on God to live a life full of Him.

LIONS OF DISTRACTIONS

CHAPTER FIVE

At the Field Museum of Natural History in Chicago, there's a display of two lions that terrorized a construction camp in Africa in 1898. These lions, known as the Man-eaters of Tsavo, developed an appetite for human flesh. It's estimated that they killed and devoured up to 135 people before being shot and killed. Imagine life in those tents—no glow of city lights, just darkness. People were likely too scared to sleep, always on high alert, weapons ready, hoping they wouldn't become the lions' next victims. Living in those conditions required constant vigilance.

Do you know there's a lion after you too? The Enemy is real. He's known as the devouring lion, and whether we believe in him or not, the Bible tells us he exists. He probably doesn't look like we imagine—no red tights or pitchfork—but the Bible describes him clearly. The word "Devil" or *diabolos* means "the slanderer" and is used 35 times in the Bible. He's referred to as Satan 54 times, the Evil One 5 times, and the Wicked One 8 times. He's a wicked, evil slanderer.

A lot of people deny the existence of a literal Devil. A Barna study found that 50% of born-again Christians believe the Devil is just a symbol of evil, and another poll showed that 65% of Christians didn't believe in a real Devil at all. This is a serious problem. We're unaware that there's a lion outside our door, waiting to devour us. He's destroyed and devoured countless lives. Living unaware makes us unprepared, and walking through life unprepared is dangerous.

The Bible tells us we have an enemy of the soul—Satan, the deceiver, the liar. He hates us because we are made in God's image, and ultimately, he hates God. His mission is to destroy anything and everything that reflects God's glory, all because of his own pride. Satan has a plan, and part of that plan is to destroy our destiny, the God-given purpose each of us carries.

The Bible often uses the word "schemes" to describe the Devil's plans. A scheme is a clever strategy used to achieve a negative end. The enemy of the soul is a master strategist, coming up with ways to infiltrate and destroy our lives. He's calculated, with plans and procedures designed to bring us down. One of his greatest tricks, as it's been said, is convincing the world that he doesn't exist.

Now, while the enemy would love to take us out completely, if he can't kill us, his next best move is to distract us. Billy Graham once said, "*Satan doesn't need for us to fall into gross sin in order to defeat us. A large dose of laziness will do the trick just as well. Put Christ first in your life, and then commit every hour of the day to Him.*" In other words, apathy, negligence, or carelessness can be just as dangerous as outright sin.

We must realize that there is opposition—both physical and spiritual—that wants to stop us from fulfilling God's purpose for our lives. If you think you have no enemies, life will surprise you sooner or later, and you'll see the spiritual battles you're up against. There are real dark spiritual forces in the world. Call them spirits or demons, they are real, and they operate in a realm beyond what our natural eyes can see.

Now, there are extremes when it comes to beliefs about spiritual forces. Some people deny their existence altogether, while others are obsessed and see them everywhere. C.S. Lewis wisely wrote, *"Satan hails the skeptic and superstitious alike. There are two equal and opposite errors into which our race can fall about the devils. One is to disbelieve in their existence. The other is to believe, and to feel an excessive and unhealthy interest in them."* Growing up in church, I saw both ends of this spectrum—people who were obsessed with demons and others who completely denied their existence. I think we need a balanced, healthy view. Yes, there are dark forces against us, but the good news is that their fight is already a defeated one.

Nevertheless, we must stay alert. The Apostle Paul wrote in his letter to the Corinthians, *"Many oppose me,"* a phrase that accurately describes the distractions and detractors we face in life. There is opposition to the Spirit of God inside you, opposition to the calling God has placed on your life, and opposition to your unique gifts, talents, and destiny. If we're not careful, we'll get distracted, take detours, and lose focus, missing out on the plans

God has for us. Distractions are at an all-time high, pulling us away from the war raging around us.

Of course, I also believe that the Spirit of God living in us is stronger than any opposition. But that doesn't mean we're free from responsibility and discipline. In fact, God is with us and for us, but He also created us to accomplish good works. The Bible says in Ephesians that we were created for good works in Him. This means God has plans and paths for us to walk and fulfill. We were designed on purpose, for a purpose.

Distractions happen to all of us. Have you ever walked or driven while distracted? For instance, I once went walking by a lake where there had been sightings of alligators. I was so focused on searching for one that I almost walked right into a massive streetlight pole! I was completely distracted. Or have you ever arrived somewhere and suddenly thought, *How did I get here?* Your mind was on everything except the route you were taking! No? Just me?

A few years ago, a popular rap song had everyone dancing to it on social media. People would play the song in their cars, open the door, and dance alongside their moving vehicles. Soon, videos popped up of people getting distracted by the camera, only to run into cars, poles, or other people. These clips got millions of views, and we all laughed at them. They were distracted. While some distractions are funny, others can be deadly.

I believe physical, emotional, mental, and spiritual distractions can be dangerous. If we aren't careful where we're going, we can end up in the wrong place. I like to put it this way: **A distracted life leads to a detracted life.** Distractions rob us of the potential our lives hold and keep us from doing all we can. When we stray from the right path, we stray from the purpose God has for us. We lose the quality of life when we end up where we aren't supposed to be. Life becomes less than what it could be when we are constantly inattentive.

Discipline is a word we may not like, but we really need it. It's about dying to what we *want* to do in order to achieve all we *desire* to be. Discipline is not easy, and self-denial never is. It can take time, tears, and sometimes even sweat and blood, but the outcome is always worth it. If we want to be healthy, we need the discipline to sweat and sometimes to bleed. If we want to grow in knowledge and wisdom, we need the discipline to put down distractions, pick up books, and study. You may have to say no to something in order to become great in one thing.

If we look at the greats in any field, we learn about their discipline. Whether it's LeBron James, Andrea Bocelli, Carlos Alcaraz, or the late Larry King, these individuals honed their craft through hours of disciplined learning, growth, and practice. **Greatness doesn't just happen.** It's the result of determination and focus. It doesn't appear when you hit the "big lights." It's cultivated in the shadows, when no one is watching. It's during those personal moments, when we decide to be better, that greatness is born. Whether we aspire to be a better man, woman, son, daughter, parent, entrepreneur, employee, lawyer, doctor, or athlete, we can become better if we stay focused and avoid distractions.

The more disciplined we are, the better equipped we are to combat not only our own internal struggles but also the distractions of the enemy of our soul. Distractions, both physical and spiritual, can derail us if we aren't careful.

Discipline and victory don't happen by accident. If we want to overcome a bad habit, a lack of focus, or sin, we need to be intentional and focused. I like to say **that if your focus is right, you'll live a purpose-filled life.** Focus not on the negatives but on the positive word of God. Focus not on your unfaithfulness but on God's faithfulness. Don't dwell on the past—focus on the present and be expectant for the future. Be mindful of your tendencies and desires. Write down the habits you need to cut out and replace them with good, healthy habits that require discipline.

We must stay aware of distractions. In one of his letters, the Apostle John, who wrote the Gospel of John, the epistles of John, and Revelation, gives us insight into how the enemy uses distractions. John, one of Jesus' closest friends, refers to himself as "the one that Jesus loved," and it's amazing how many times he mentions this. When John wrote 1 John, he was older, writing with the wisdom of experience, like a father to his children.

In 1 John 2:15, he says, "*Do not love the world or the things in the world. If anyone loves the world, the love of the Father is not in him. For all that is in the world—the desires of the flesh and the desires of the eyes and pride of life—is not from the Father but is from the world. And the world is passing away along with its desires, but whoever does the will of God abides forever.*"

John wants us to be aware and focused. Be careful. Live with the knowledge of these distractions. When he says, "do not love the world," he's talking about the systems, values, and standards of the world. Don't love the way the world is set up. The Message paraphrase puts it like this in 1 John 2:15: "*Don't love the world's ways. Don't love the world's goods. Love of the world squeezes out love for the Father."*

I love that last line. The love of the world squeezes out love for the Father. And in turn, love for the Father squeezes out love for the world. In other words, don't focus on all the world promises to give you—focus on the Father! Squeeze out love for the world!

John tells us about the three primary ways the enemy of our souls attacks: the **Lust of the Flesh**, the **Lust of the Eyes,** and the **Pride of Life**. These are essential to understand because they represent the core methods by which our souls can be distracted.

Let's break them down and see how they affect us:

Lust of the Flesh relates to the *pleasures* we desire. It's the craving for things that make us feel good in the moment.

Lust of the Eyes deals with the *possessions* we want. It's the allure of having what we see and desire.

Pride of Life is about the *positions* we crave. It's the temptation to be important, to seek validation through status and power.

We see these three tactics at work in both the story of Adam and Eve and in Jesus 'temptation in the desert. They are major distractions:

Lust of the Flesh makes you want to indulge in things that give immediate gratification.

Lust of the Eyes tempts you to desire what you see, whether you need it or not.

Pride of Life pushes you to seek recognition, to crave positions and places of influence.

In other words, they boil down to three core thoughts:

"I want to feel."

"I want to have."

"I want to be."

Be aware of these distractions. When your heart, mind, and soul begin to desire satisfaction through fleeting pleasures, when you find yourself fascinated by things you shouldn't have, or when you crave recognition from people or places that don't really matter, you're being led astray. Focusing on the wrong things will cause you to miss your path.

The war in our souls, the missing fire in our world, and the false perceptions of success, fame, and happiness all stem from falling for distractions—from ourselves, the world, and dark spiritual forces. We must stay disciplined to remain on course, pursuing inner peace, freedom, and clarity. It's often said that a lack of discipline becomes a lid on our lives, preventing us from reaching our potential. This is absolutely true. We must be aware, focused, and recognize the schemes against our souls. Every decision we make matters, and what we choose to engage with will shape the health of our soul.

Paul's advice to his protégé Timothy is relevant for us today: *"Discipline yourself for the purpose of godliness."* If we want to see our minds, hearts, and emotions healthy, it's going to take discipline. If we want to see our cities transformed, it will require focus and control. Are you in control of your thoughts, your will, and your emotions?

One of the most important disciplines we can develop is a love and habit of reading our Bibles. Warren Wiersbe, in his classic book *The Strategy of Satan*, writes, "I have found that trusting God's promises and laying hold of His Word will quench these fiery darts." He emphasizes our need for the Word of God. He writes, "We cannot stop Satan from throwing the darts, but we can keep them from starting a fire. The important thing is to quench that dart immediately. Instantly look to Christ by faith, recall some promise of the Word, and believe it. Otherwise, the fire will start to spread, and if you add fuel to it, it will get beyond your control. Your feelings will get aroused and upset, and before long, Satan will be in control."

We must put some of the basic and age-old disciplines into practice: prayer, meditating on God's Word, and worship. Practicing these disciplines will help us feed our spirit and starve our flesh. As the old saying goes, what you feed will grow, and what you starve dies. Galatians reminds us that *"the fruit of the Spirit is self-control."* In other words, if we can't control ourselves, we will be controlled by our own desires. It's time to focus. There's a war in our cities, a fight to engage in. We must be awake and aware, because the fire is fading, and the enemy is prowling.

The Briefing Room

Step Five - Attention

Take one minute to identify your biggest distractions. What are some things that are taking your time and focus away from what you should be doing? Some time to relax, laugh, and have fun is absolutely necessary, but I'm talking about detrimental time and energy being wasted on destructive things. Ask God to help you pay attention and stay sharp.

THE DOOR IS OPEN

CHAPTER SIX

I hate frogs. I truly do. They're tiny demons. When God wanted to teach the Egyptians a lesson, what did He send? Exactly—frogs. You're welcome. In our neighborhood, these creatures are everywhere, especially during the rainy summer nights. You can hear them croaking in the water preserve behind our house—thousands of them. We find them at our gate when we get home, on our doors, and sometimes even on our cars. It's a real problem. *Lord, are You trying to teach us a lesson too? Help!*

Every so often, we leave the sliding glass door open briefly to let the dogs out or take out the trash. The problem is, we live in a jungle—South Miami is full of iguanas, ducks, mosquitoes, and, of course, frogs. A couple of years ago, we had a few nights where we found frogs inside our house—three of them! It was one of the most disturbing things I've had to deal with. I detest them.

Since I'm the man of the house, it was my job to get them out. I tried to be brave, but on the inside, I was dying. You can't even imagine the acrobatic stunts I pulled trying to trap them and get them out without hurting them. Every time they moved, I'd jump back in terror. Diana was screaming, I was screaming, and I kept feeling like one had jumped on me. You know that feeling? It's the worst! It took a while, but I finally got them all out.

What I learned from that horrific ordeal is this: an open door invites unwanted intruders. If I keep leaving the door open, the frogs will keep coming in. The best way to keep them out is to close the door. You better believe I'm careful now. Our door is barely open when we go in and out during rainy nights. We don't want any more frogs coming in, and we've become mindful of when they're most active.

The problem with the human soul is similar. We often leave the door of our minds, wills, and emotions wide open, allowing things to come in and take root. Unless we fix it, these intruders—negative thoughts, emotions, and feelings—will keep coming in, robbing us of peace, joy, hope, and faith. **How's the door to your soul today?** Are you allowing just any thought, feeling, or emotion to linger and make a home inside?

This frog problem got me thinking: *What am I allowing into my soul?* Is the door to my soul open, and if so, what am I doing about it? There have been times when I've been quick to deal with negative emotions and thoughts and get them out. But there have also been times when I've allowed them to linger longer than they should. I've realized that when I allow these things to stay, they start to steal my joy, peace, and hope. I should have dealt with them sooner. I shouldn't have let them stick around.

My Biggest Enemy

The bottom line is this: **you can't transform what you tolerate**. If I want a soul full of life, faith, hope, and joy, I need to close the door on anything that tries to rob it. The truth is, we can't change what we allow. In fact, what we tolerate often accelerates. What I mean is, the longer we allow something to stay, the more comfortable it becomes, and the harder it is to get rid of. We see this with children all the time—whatever behavior parents permit, the child continues to exhibit.

If we keep allowing negative, faithless thoughts and emotions to settle in our souls, they will soon take over. Those bad, negative feelings will grow faster than we realize and will take control of our lives. In the book of Revelation, John the Apostle receives a vision from Jesus, who tells him to write letters to seven churches. In Revelation 2:20, Jesus addresses the church in Thyatira. He commends them for their love, faith, and service but quickly points out something He's not pleased with: *"But I have this against you, that you tolerate that woman Jezebel, who calls herself a prophetess and is teaching and seducing my servants to practice sexual immorality and to eat food sacrificed to idols."*

Whoa! There was a woman named Jezebel in the church, evil, wicked, and faithless. Yet, the church allowed her to teach, even though she was leading people into sin and destruction. The church was doing well in many areas, but in this one, they were failing—and it was costing them more than they realized. In other words, *their door was open*. They had allowed Jezebel to come in and stay.

Sometimes, it's not what comes into our lives that causes the most harm, but what we allow to stay.

If we're honest, we've all had moments or seasons where we tolerate certain things in our souls—sin, bad habits, toxic thoughts, negative traits, or even addictions. If we're not careful, these things become an open door for the "frogs" of our soul to creep in. And this can happen to anyone, even believers. We can be saved, baptized, active in church, and doing well in many areas, but our souls can still be affected by faithlessness and hopelessness.

Although I don't believe that a frog—or an intruding thought, emotion, or feeling in your soul—will rob you of salvation, it can certainly steal your potential. These intruders can prevent you from living a thriving life here on Earth. The Apostle Paul, in Ephesians 4:28, says, *"Do not give the devil a foothold."* In other words, don't give the devil any opportunity to get a grip on your life. Many of us, whether knowingly or unknowingly, give him a space in our hearts, and that foothold can soon become a stronghold.

Walk It Out

What are strongholds? A stronghold is essentially a prison or a fortress. An open door—an area in your life where you allow negativity to creep in—can quickly become a prison. Open doors leave us trapped. Often, we don't even realize we've built prison walls with the things we've allowed and tolerated. Uncontrolled thoughts, emotions, or desires can imprison our lives, leading us down paths we never intended to take.

As I think about the war on our souls and what we allow to take root, I've realized that our greatest enemy is often ourselves—our "inner me." The choices we make, what we tolerate, and what we don't seek help for can be our biggest downfall. When we allow temptation, negativity, or faithlessness to enter and dwell in our souls, it doesn't just stop there. The temptation becomes a choice, and that choice becomes a trap. Today, many of us are trapped in our troubles.

You don't need to be behind physical bars to be imprisoned. Many of us are living in prisons within our own minds, wills, and emotions. The intruder—whether a negative thought, emotion, or godless desire—has come into our souls and made itself at home. We didn't kick it out or seek help, and now it has made itself comfortable, living like it owns the place. As a result, we find ourselves trapped, imprisoned by our own thoughts, emotions, and decisions.

It feels like being stuck in an invisible cage—on the outside, everything may seem fine, but inside, you know you're not free. The weight is constant, pressing down on your chest, making it hard to breathe deeply. It's a heaviness that doesn't lift, even when you smile or go about your daily routine. The prison walls may not be visible, but you feel them closing in, shrinking your world until even the smallest tasks feel impossible.

Every step feels like you're dragging chains behind you, as if you're always moving through quicksand, never able to get ahead. There's a deep sense of isolation, even in a crowded room, because no one else can see the struggle going on within. You want to break free, but the more you try, the more trapped you feel. Hope fades, and it seems like the walls of this prison will never fall.

There are many types of prisons:

The prison of depression, where despair and discouragement from difficult circumstances keep us bound.

The prison of trauma, where past abuse or neglect has left lasting emotional scars.

The prison of bad habits or addictions, built over time, that we haven't sought help for.

The prisons of anxiety, stress, shame, and guilt, which keep us locked in cycles of self-condemnation.

The longer we allow these thoughts, emotions, and feelings to linger, the more confusion, guilt, and shame we experience. Over time, this can lead to self-condemnation and frustration, and living in this kind of stronghold robs us of the joy and freedom God intends for us. I don't believe this is the life God meant for us to live. He doesn't desire for us to live oppressed.

I don't want to become my own worst enemy. You and I need to recognize what we've allowed and tolerated in our souls. Some of these things have been with us for so long, they've become part of our identity. We tell ourselves, *"I'll always be the less loved one,"* or *"I'll never be free."* These negative thoughts have taken such deep root that they now shape how we speak, think, and live. If we continue to leave the doors open, I believe we'll find ourselves in one of three outcomes:

Distressed: Overwhelmed by the onslaught of negative emotions and thoughts, we become distressed and anxious daily.

Isolated: Feeling ashamed, guilty, or tired, we begin to isolate ourselves from family and friends—something that is never healthy.

Oppressed: We end up living under the rule of these feelings and thoughts, never enjoying life to the fullest. We may be saved, but we're sad; believers, but bitter; heaven-bound, but feeling like we're in hell.

The Big Three

When we study the scriptures, we find that we really have three primary enemies. Paul explains this in Ephesians 2:1-3, "And you were dead in the trespasses and sins in which you once walked, following the course of this world, following the prince of the power of the air, the spirit that is now at work in the sons of disobedience—among whom we all once lived in the passions of our flesh, carrying out the desires of the body and the mind." From this passage, we learn that the three main enemies we face are:

The World

The Devil

The Flesh

These three forces work constantly against us, trying to keep us in a prison. There is a war for our worship, and the traps of the world, the devil, and our flesh can leave us in bondage, oppression, and captivity within our souls.

Here's how the "Big Three" work:

The World surrounds you, tempting you to compromise your values, morals, worship, and standards.

Satan comes against you, trying to deceive and oppress you, leading you away from God's truth.

The Flesh is within you, luring you with cravings, desires, lust, and unresolved trauma.

But when we learn to deny these temptations and not feed them, we begin to avoid the pitfalls that trap our souls. You'll notice when the world, the flesh, and Satan have taken your eyes off Jesus. Billy Graham once said, "You have a thirst to be free from those things that enslave you. Freedom from the insecurity and uncertainty that you feel. You have this thirst because God created you in His image. He created you for Himself. You have a spirit that will live forever, and that's the part of you that thirsts for eternal freedom."

If the "Big Three"—the world, the flesh, and Satan—have caused any intimidation or disruption in your life, don't forget that we have three mighty helpers: **the Father, the Son, and the Spirit**. These three, who are truly one, provide the strength we need to overcome. The more we lean on God and distance ourselves from the world, the flesh, and Satan, the fewer intruders we'll have in our souls. I once heard a powerful and true statement: **What you feed grows, what you starve dies.**

I'm constantly making decisions to starve the world, the flesh, and Satan. When I find myself too immersed in the news, pop culture, or meaningless distractions of the world, I take action to remove those influences from my life. While it's important to stay informed about essential world events, there's no need to let the world consume my time and attention. I starve those distractions.

The same goes for the flesh and Satan. When the desires of the flesh become too loud or when Satan's lies start replaying in my mind, I actively work to silence them. The flesh, with its cravings, lusts, and traumas, is subdued when I begin to starve it. Sometimes, I fast—abstaining from certain foods, social media, or other distractions for a few days. **Starve the giants, and they fall**. Satan, with his deceptions and lies, is resisted when I fill my mind with Scripture and my time with prayer, instead of letting intrusive thoughts run wild.

The world, the flesh, and Satan only have as much power over us as we allow them to. In Jesus Christ, they are defeated foes, but we must be intentional about not letting them creep back into our lives through open doors. **Starve the Big Three**, and allow the **real Big Three**—the Father, Son, and Spirit—to bring you life, freedom, and help.

Jesus came not only to save our spirits but to free our souls as well. Today, make the decision to close the door on these enemies. I understand that many times, we can't do this alone.

That's why I thank God for pastors, mentors, therapists, and doctors. Decide today to take action—call someone, meet with someone who will help you clean out your soul. Get rid of the frogs. There is so much more for you and me.

Close the door on distractions, and walk into the open spaces of your destiny.

The Briefing Room

Step Six - Agree

Take one minute to see what negative and faithless thoughts or ideas you have let linger in your life for too long. Make a decision to disagree with them and agree with what God says. Begin to say "yes" to everything the Bible speaks and promises over you, and shut the door on all that the enemy has said, is saying, or will say.

PART 2:

HEAL THE SOUL

BREAKING FREE

CHAPTER SEVEN

The famous novel **1984** by George Orwell has been widely discussed and analyzed for its prophetic depiction of the future. Written in 1949, it's considered a classic and has received global attention for its portrayal of a totalitarian society controlled by the government and constantly watched by "Big Brother." The novel describes what life might look like in 1984, showing how civilization is absolutely controlled, manipulated, and enslaved by a totalitarian regime. It's a fascinating and thought-provoking read.

In the book, a character named O'Brien, representing the oppressive government, speaks to and tortures Winston, who symbolizes the oppressed society. O'Brien explains how the Party's goal is to control humanity by eliminating all positive emotions and leaving only negative feelings. The aim is to completely break the human mind and force total submission to Big Brother. One of the most famous lines from the novel comes during this moment when O'Brien tells Winston: *"If you want a picture of the future, imagine a boot stamping on a human face—forever."*

This quote paints a bleak picture of unrelenting power, control, and oppression. It suggests a future in which the state endlessly oppresses its people, leaving no hope for freedom or change. The novel's society is depicted as dumbed down, indoctrinated, programmed, drugged, and permanently controlled.

I was reminded of this quote because it reflects what happens to many of us when we feel oppressed by the wars in our own souls. Perhaps the battle has left you feeling defeated, with no hope of freedom from the issues of your past. Maybe distractions and enemies seem to have taken over your soul, and you keep giving your attention and worship to the wrong things. But I believe there is a path to freedom and healing for our souls.

We've discussed the war for our soul—the constant battle for our mind, body, and spirit, with distractions and enemies vying for our worship and attention. We talked about the importance of closing the door to these enemies, and that's a daily step we all need to take. I'm with you in this fight—I'm not exempt from it. Together, we close the doors we've too often left open, allowing arrows to pierce our souls.

But the path to healing begins with cleaning up the mess these enemies have left in our souls—mess that has left us feeling oppressed, beaten down, and hopeless. For some of us, when we think about the future, it feels like we're being stomped on, like that boot from Orwell's **1984**—trapped, unable to move forward. Our minds, emotions, and souls are weighed down by enslaving thoughts, negative patterns, and lies we've allowed to take root. These thoughts have marked a path in our souls that now must be healed.

We've all lost some battles, taken our eyes off the right things, and focused on the wrong ones. No one goes through life without arrows coming toward their soul. We've left doors open, and today we may be mentally, emotionally, or spiritually oppressed. If we want to restore the health of our souls, one of the first places to start is our minds—our thought life.

Take the Wheel

Our mind is the steering wheel of our life. **As we think, so we go.** It doesn't matter what we want to do or where we want to go if our minds are moving in the opposite direction. Pastor Craig Groeschel once said, *"Your life will always move in the direction of your strongest thoughts,"* and I believe that's absolutely true. Our strongest thoughts dictate the direction of our lives. You can't keep thinking negative, defeated thoughts and expect to move toward victory. You can't live a free life if your mind is enslaved.

Let's make a decision today. Let's clean out our minds and get rid of those toxic thoughts. It will take time, work, and possibly help from others, but I truly believe there's a healthy soul in your future. You will no longer be kicked down.

What thoughts are ruling our minds? Is it shame, guilt, abuse, hurt, betrayal, insecurities, or feelings of inferiority? For many of us, our past still haunts our minds and dictates our future. The past is like that boot that keeps kicking us down, whispering lies: *You're no good. You'll never be good. You're damaged goods.*

You've been abused. You're too dumb. You're a hypocrite. You'll never amount to anything.

The mind is incredibly powerful—it can be a tool for both good and evil. There are things the mind can endure and processes that are quite remarkable. While the body can withstand only so much, the mind can suffer for a lifetime. Charles Spurgeon once said, *"The mind can descend far lower than the body, for in it there are bottomless pits. The flesh can bear only a certain number of wounds and no more, but the soul can bleed in ten thousand ways, and die over and over again each hour."*

If there's one place where the enemy of our soul—Satan—loves to attack, it's the mind. That's why it's critical to close the doors to these attacks and start breaking free from the things that have consumed our souls. Make the decision today: *Enough is enough.* The thoughts that have haunted you, held you captive, and dictated your life will no longer enslave you. You can have a free soul that lives and explores all that God has for you. Don't let these thoughts continue to control your life. It's time to change your thinking, one thought at a time.

Researchers at Columbia University found that the average person makes about 70 conscious decisions a day. That adds up to 25,550 decisions a year and, over 70 years, a staggering

1,788,500 decisions in a lifetime. Some decisions, like what to wear, seem small, while others, like who to marry, have lasting impact. But all our decisions matter more than we realize.

The French philosopher Albert Camus said, *"Life is the sum of all your choices."* In other words, our choices shape who we are. We must pay close attention to our decisions and choices. If our decisions matter this much, we must be cautious about the thoughts, emotions, and ideas we allow into our minds. What we allow into our minds will ultimately affect our decisions. If we don't guard our thoughts, anything can take root in our souls.

Dr. Athena Staik of *Psych Central* explains that our thoughts create "inner standards" that spark neurochemical processes governing our choices and actions. Every thought we have causes changes in our brain—there's no such thing as a random thought.

Idea War

There's an actual war going on, and the enemy wants to use our thoughts to negatively impact our reality. The world around us—the ads, images, videos, and countless distractions—are constantly filling our minds, taking up space in our souls to distract us. We must be ready to fight back.

Growing up in church, I often heard the term *spiritual warfare*. In some circles, it was all about chasing demons. We were taught to pray against them, to be vigilant in looking out for them. Some people became overly paranoid about demons, but I always believed, and still do, that Jesus is greater than any demon. There was an underlying belief that if you were going through something, it must be because of a demonic influence.

After much reflection, I've come to realize that while demons are real and have power, we tend to blame them far too often. A demon might introduce a thought, but it's what we allow ourselves to dwell on that causes the most harm. You can pray against demons, but unless you deal with what's lingering in your mind, true freedom won't come. If we want to be free in our lives, we need to be healed in our minds.

The spiritual world is absolutely real, more real than our physical world. I'm not denying the existence of spiritual beings, but most of the time, the things that hold us back aren't demons—they're the thoughts in our own heads. In other words, **spiritual warfare often begins in the mind**. The greatest spiritual battle we fight is located there. But here's the good news: we are not powerless or defenseless against these thoughts.

To be free from the onslaught against our souls and to free our minds from years of wrong thinking, we need a greater source of power. You and I can't defeat these thoughts alone. We all know how it works: the less we want to think about something, the more it consumes us. The truth is, we'll constantly be bombarded with thoughts and ideas. But we don't have to be defeated by them. **Thanks be to God—He gives us a way out**. Today, we need to trust in God's perfect power, not our imperfect abilities. We win the battle by trusting in God's power, not our performance.

We will stumble, and we will fall, but the Bible says that the righteous get up again. Trust that as you lean into God, you'll begin to break free. While we are physically weak and frail, we don't have to be weak in spirit. The spiritual weapons we use in warfare are powerful and mighty, given to us by God. As Paul told the Corinthian church: "*For though we walk in the flesh, we are not waging war according to the flesh. For the weapons of our warfare are not of the flesh but have divine power to destroy strongholds*" (2 Corinthians 10:3-4).

In the second letter Paul wrote to the church in Corinth, chapter 10 holds some incredibly powerful truths. As we read earlier, Paul explains that the war we're engaged in is not physical. He continues in verses 4-5: "*We destroy arguments and every lofty opinion raised against the knowledge of God, and take every thought captive to obey Christ.*"

Paul reveals a profound truth: we can dismantle and bring down thoughts and ideas that oppose God's truth. **We are at war for freedom in our souls, and that battle is fought in our thoughts.**

In Paul's time, just like in ours, there were many voices teaching and spreading ideologies that went against God's truth. Humanism, existentialism, pride, worldly wisdom, cults, and false religions were all emerging during Paul's era, just as they are today. People were crafting ideas about life, its purpose, and human existence based on false premises that didn't align with God's Word. Paul urges believers not to let their minds be subjugated by these false claims.

The portrayal of the Christian life as a military operation is common in Paul. It occurs in at least eleven other places in his letters. What is interesting here is how he handles the idea of a military operation not just against the principalities and powers of darkness (as in Ephesians 6), but against actual human enemies. The first thing of importance to note is that the whole depiction here is drawn from the language of siege warfare, beginning with "weapons" in verse 4. This word actually means "siege engines." This is very significant because siegecraft is an entirely offensive operation. Spiritual warfare at its heart is never defensive but always offensive. Why is it that we picture spiritual warfare as believers huddled behind shields while the enemy hurls his spears at us? No, the truth is that the enemy is in a besieged city which we are aggressively attacking!

Many words in these verses have various meanings but can be translated as terms of siegecraft: "demolition" (verse 4), "fortresses" or "strongholds" (verse 4), "bastions of argumentation" (verse 4), "raised rampart" (verse 5), "carry off into captivity" (verse 5), "battle plan" or "opposing design" (verse 5), "subjection" or "submission" (verse 5), "be at the ready" or "like a soldier on standby" (verse 6), and "insubordination" (verse 6).

If we translated verses 4-6 using these military meanings (which would be readily understandable to all of Paul's readers), the translation would read as follows: "For the siege engines of our military campaign are not the siege engines of the world, but are powerful for the demolition of fortresses. We demolish bastions of argumentation and every raised rampart that sets itself up against the knowledge of God; we carry off into captivity every battle plan in subjection to Christ; and we stand at the ready to punish any insubordination once your subjection is complete." That puts a different perspective on it! Even though this is not the normal translation, all these secondary meanings would be in the minds of his readers, as he adds one figure of speech onto another.

We have different weapons—spiritual weapons that are powerful and divinely effective. We are to fight in a way that brings down strongholds of lies and false thinking.

The War of Ideas

Some of us have been caught up in this war, and perhaps we've lost a battle or two. The ideas of the world may have gained an upper hand in how we think and process life. We are living in an idea war. Many ideas in the world exalt themselves against the knowledge of God—they are puffed up, arrogant, narcissistic, and utterly false.

Ungodly thoughts and ideologies abound today, such as the belief that man is his own god, that we can make choices without God's wisdom, or that enlightenment can be achieved without Scripture. Other ideas, like denying God's existence, the concept of evolution, the breakdown of gender, and more, are also widespread. These thoughts are not only worldly and false but demonic in nature. If we're not careful, they can take root and hold us captive, oppressing us like prisoners of war.

When we lose battle after battle in this war of ideas, we start to lose sight of the truth. We begin to view ourselves, our world, and even God through the lens of man's opinions, philosophies, theories, and lies, rather than through the truth of God's Word. However, when we come to the saving knowledge that Jesus is the Son of God, who died and rose again to save us, we realize that **He is the ultimate truth**. Jesus is the way, the truth, and the life. When we surrender our thoughts and ideas to His ways, we find life, and life to the fullest. This is why we don't live according to how the world thinks or labels us. If we do, we risk living a life based on faulty thinking and heading in the wrong direction.

Spiritual Warfare in the Mind

I want to suggest that perhaps **spiritual warfare** is less about battling demons and more about battling our thoughts, ideas, and lies that rise above God's truth. When we use God's Word, we wield the power to destroy strongholds, break down false fortresses, and escape the tombs that have gripped our souls.

This is what Paul is trying to tell us: through the Holy Spirit, we have the power to break out of mental prisons. **Our thought**

life directly impacts our spiritual life. It's crucial to capture your thoughts before they captivate you.

If spiritual warfare begins in the mind, we need to understand that there are three primary ways the enemy attacks our thoughts:

False Thoughts: The enemy tries to convince us that God's Word isn't true.

Failure Thoughts: The enemy whispers lies, telling us we've made too many mistakes.

Fear Thoughts: The enemy breeds fear in us, making us feel inadequate or terrified of the unknown.

Get Out!

Paul tells us to "*take every thought captive."* The term "*take captive"* is a war term, meaning to seize or capture with an offensive weapon. In other words, Paul is urging us to go on the offensive against our thoughts. No more letting our minds, or the world's false and arrogant ideas, rule over us. No more being held hostage to godless chatter, demonic lies, or negative self-talk. No more being enslaved by ungodly thinking or antichrist ways.

It's time to take action! Get those thoughts out—every day, every hour, every minute, and if necessary, every second. Say it out loud if you must: "**You are a lie, and God is truth!**"

It's time to expel the godless thoughts that have invaded our souls. These lies have even infiltrated the church and are spreading like wildfire. But we do not conform. We stand firm on God's Word. It may not always feel good in the moment, but the truth is good for us in the long run. The more we remind ourselves of God's truths, the freer we become.

In John 8:36, Jesus says, "*If the Son sets you free, you are free indeed.*" You don't have to continue living in sin, faithlessness, hopelessness, or destruction. We need to break free and find healing and wholeness in our minds, bodies, and souls. I firmly believe we were created to live big, free lives.

Make the decision today to start taking steps toward healing, even if it's just one step. Decide that you will live free—free in your mind and soul. You were created for more than living enslaved to thoughts, ideas, and emotions that hold you captive.

Break free from the self-destructive thoughts that life can't get better for you or your family and friends. Break free from the anxiety that wants to drown you in worry. Anxiety is having faith that the bad thing will happen. I believe God wants to heal us.

God wants healing for your weary soul. It's time to break free from the pretense, abuse, unforgiveness, toxic traits, mental strongholds, persistent temptations, fleshly desires, hidden wounds, anger, pride, laziness—whatever it is, break free! Jesus died and rose again so that you and I can live in victory and in total freedom.

The Briefing Room

Step Seven - Charge

Take one minute to get on the offensive today. Pick up the sword God has given us and start to memorize some verses. Decide that every morning you will begin by charging toward the army against you. Pastor Craig Groeschel has some powerful biblical morning declarations that have helped me. Write some of your own down today as you walk in victory.

PRESS RESET

CHAPTER EIGHT

It seems like there's a new product or gadget coming out every day. Recently, the latest iPhone was released. My wife and I both have iPhones, and we love them. We had an upgrade available—who doesn't love upgrades?! We weren't sure if we'd upgrade our phones, but they suddenly started acting strange. Is it just me, or does your iPhone battery and phone seem to slow down every time a new one comes out? That's how they get us.

Well, they got us. We went for the upgrade. As we were getting our brand-new phones, we had to turn in the old ones.

Before doing that, we made sure to transfer all our information—pictures, files, everything. Once everything was moved, it was time to turn in our old phones for some compensation toward the new ones. The young man helping us told us we needed to reset our old phones to factory settings.

If you've ever owned an iPhone, you know how this works. You go into settings and click reset, but before doing so, you need to make sure everything—your personal files, pictures, etc.—is backed up. Otherwise, you lose it all. Every message, picture, email, note—gone! When you hit reset, the phone returns to its original state, as if it's just been unboxed. Everything is wiped clean, and it's like starting fresh with a brand-new phone. Have you ever wished life had a reset button like that? Have you ever wanted to start over in your personal life? Maybe from a past decision, career choice, marriage, or business venture?

I believe we can start over in many areas, but it begins with our spiritual life. Many of us wish we could take back things we've said or done or feel bad about past decisions. Some of us feel less than qualified to be believers because of our past. Have you ever felt far from God, like He's a million miles away?

Many of us have felt that way—distant from God. Something happens that sidetracks us. We make wrong decisions, bad choices, and things go wrong. Life feels off track, and it seems like our connection with heaven has been lost. Life can leave our faith in decline and our feelings in disarray. Our faith seems lost, absent, and our emotions are all over the place. We're sad, angry, confused, disillusioned. Life often leaves us with faith in one place and feelings in another.

I've been there. There have been times in my life when I've felt mentally exhausted, emotionally distraught, and as if I were just going through the motions in life, marriage, relationships, and even church. We keep moving forward day after day without ever hitting reset. We continue doing the same things without addressing the root of our struggles. Many of us have adopted the traditions of religion, but God desires a relationship.

I know that phrase—"relationship, not religion"—has been mocked because it's been repeated so many times, but that's not the point. Christianity is a religion, but what I'm talking about is that many of us have a set of rituals, but those rituals aren't producing life.

We go to church, we go to work, we pray when we're in need, but we're disconnected and disenchanted with life and with God. We need to understand that God desires **relationship**. He wants to be included in every detail of our lives, to be with us in the highs and lows, the mountaintops, and the valleys. He walks with us through the darkest, most painful moments. He wants us to live with Him, talk with Him, and lean on Him. And if you've stumbled, if you feel unworthy, lost, or confused, know this: God is not distant. In a moment, He can forgive, restore, and revive you. God is calling us to reset. It's time to start again.

Time to Thrive

God's desire for you and me is to live **full lives**. In John 10:10, Jesus says, *"The enemy comes to steal, kill, and destroy, but I have come that you may have life, and life to the fullest."* In other words, don't let the disappointments, setbacks, and confusion rob you of life. Instead, let them create a deeper desire to explore the divine. Ask God, *"Why?"* and invite Him into your questions. As you do, life becomes an adventure filled with surprises, lessons, and blessings. Life becomes full, not empty.

I love a statement I heard many years ago: *"We were not created to survive, but to thrive!"* That has become a life motto for me. I truly believe God created and designed us to live lives walking in the full potential and plans He has set for us. Yet, so often, we fall into a survival mentality—barely getting by. This shows up in our attitudes, behaviors, and even in our demeanor.

But I don't believe that's what God desires for you, and it's not why He created us. Begin to live again, begin to dream again!

I'm not saying life won't be challenging, difficult, or full of pain and grief. Life can be absolutely brutal at times, leaving us breathless and devastated. But what I am saying is that I believe God designed and empowered us to thrive, even as we navigate life's challenges. God wants you and me to be full of life again. He wants to reset, revive, and reignite the fire in our souls. He wants us to walk in the purposes, plans, and will He has for us—no matter what has happened.

The word **reset** means "to set back to its initial state, to set again, or to set anew." I love that definition. It's such a powerful concept when applied to our lives. We go back to the initial state God designed for us. Maybe we need an adjustment after failure. Maybe, now that we recognize we are in the middle of a spiritual war, we need to reset the eyes of our soul. All of us have the chance to reset our lives with God. We can stop following and chasing the fleeting things of this world. We can quit chasing the wind, stop living for what is temporary and vain.

Perhaps you didn't even realize you were in a war. Imagine waking up one day, stepping outside your house, and finding yourself in the middle of chaos, destruction, and terror. You realize your city is at war. What do you do? You pivot. You change direction. Maybe you were headed to the gym or work, but now you know you need to get help, take cover, and arm yourself. You need a reset.

We are in a spiritual war, and there is no more time for excuses or living oblivious to the battles within our souls. If we've been wasting time, losing battles, the good news is that **God is the God of fresh starts**. He gives hope to the hopeless, direction to the lost, and help to those in need. When you live with God, life is full of resets.

It's time to thrive. You and I can no longer live as victims, defined by our past or our flesh. We serve a good God who is for us, who is with us, and who has already won the war. Now we walk it out. Living with awareness, we can be prepared, full of hope and joy, knowing that **we will not lose**. You were not created to survive—you were created to thrive. **Reset your mentality today.**

Taking Inventory

If you've ever worked in retail or know someone who has, you're probably familiar with inventory days. These are the days when the entire store—employees and all—are tasked with counting, ordering, organizing, and putting everything in its place. Corporations want to make sure they know what they have—their assets, their valuables. It's a time to reset and reorganize.

I believe it's incredibly beneficial to take time to do a **personal inventory** of your own life. Take a few hours, or even a day, to ask yourself tough questions. Grab a journal and take stock of your values, your assets, your life. Reorganize, reorder, and reset. It's important to ask ourselves: *How am I living? What have I neglected lately?* This includes every area—spiritual, physical, mental, and emotional. *Am I going in the wrong direction? Have I let the eyes of my soul wander? Am I making the best use of my time?*

Reflecting, reviewing, and analyzing is essential. What I've learned is that **what you never review, you can never renew**. If you don't take the time to examine your life, you'll never make the steps to improve it. Billy Graham once said, "*It's not a waste of time to examine our lives and admit that we need to make some changes—if we're honest about actually doing it."* It's never a waste of time! In fact, the real waste is continuing to do the same things while expecting different results.

We've all heard the saying, "*Those who don't learn from the past are condemned to repeat it.*" And it's true. We must look at our past, and the past of others, to learn what has led to destruction and what has led to success. Some of us are wasting time in our relationships, marriages, businesses, spiritual lives, or education because we haven't taken the time to reflect, review, and figure out how we can do better.

The writer of Psalm 119 takes inventory of his own life when he writes, "*I pondered the direction of my life, and I turned to follow your laws. I will hurry, without delay, to obey your commands.*" (Psalm 119:59-60 NKJV). To **ponder** means to reflect, evaluate, and review. *How is my life? Am I following your ways?* When you review, you can reset. And when you reset, the best resets come from God. He is the designer, artist, architect, creator, and organizer of life. No one sets things in order better than God. But if you want God to reset your life, you first need to give Him your life.

The prophet Joel says, "*Rend your heart and not your garments. Return to the Lord your God, for He is gracious and compassionate, slow to anger and abounding in love, and He relents from sending calamity*" (Joel 2:13 NIV). Until you hand your life to God, you still hold onto it.

In fact, some of the best inventory comes from asking the Holy Spirit to show you the areas in your heart that need a fresh start. Proverbs 21:12 says, "People may be right in their own eyes, but the Lord examines their heart." That's a good posture and position to have. Lord, will You search our hearts and examine our intentions that we may be pure and healthy from the inside out.

If we refuse to take inventory of ourselves, we may live the rest of our lives in a false reality. A friend of mine, Phil Mion, who is a pastor in our church, says that the opposite of self-awareness is self-denial, and I think that is absolutely true. In other words, refusing to face the reality of who we are can cause us to live in such a way that we become a danger to ourselves and those we love. For example, take Apple founder and inventor Steve Jobs and his "Reality Distortion Field." Jobs had such passion and power that he could convince himself and others of almost anything, leading to significant successes. Yet, his lack of self-awareness also led to manipulation and strained relationships. This serves as a cautionary tale about how a lack of self-awareness can create a distorted reality, impacting not only ourselves but also those around us.

We should pray like the Psalmist prayed in Psalm 139:23-24: "Search me, God, and know my heart; test me and know my anxious thoughts. See if there is any offensive way in me, and lead me in the way everlasting." True self-awareness will lead to full transformation. When we press reset to who we were before we met Jesus and now take steps to become more like Jesus.

Power Thinking

We often speak of the Apostle Paul, but we must remember that he struggled too. That's encouraging because if the greatest evangelist and church planter ever struggled, then we're going to be okay! In Romans 7, Paul writes, "*For what I want to do, I do not do, but what I hate, I do... What a wretched man I am! Who will rescue me from this body of death? Thanks be to God, who delivers me through Jesus Christ our Lord!"* Wow! From this passage, we can see that Paul struggled in his Christian life. He had issues with doing what he wanted and not doing what he knew was right. He went back and forth—he even seemed a little crazy sometimes. Good news for me, because I feel crazy sometimes too!

Paul understood the importance of the mind. He knew how powerful our thoughts are, and that, with God, we can do so much! God doesn't just want us to have **positive thinking**—He wants us to have **powerful thinking**. We're called to live this new life in Jesus.

In Romans 12, Paul writes: "*Therefore, I urge you, brothers and sisters, in view of God's mercy, to offer your bodies as a living sacrifice, holy and pleasing to God—this is your true and proper worship. Do not conform to the pattern of this world, but be transformed by the renewing of your mind. Then you will be able to test and approve what God's will is—His good, pleasing, and perfect will.*"

Now, I've had my own struggles, especially with driving in Miami. It can be quite an adventure! I've driven down the Palmetto Expressway and seen people putting on lipstick, eating, and talking on the phone—all while driving. Has anyone else seen this? Some people are multitasking geniuses. And let's be honest, using turn signals seems optional in Miami! Driving here can be quite an experience.

My wife Diana, on the other hand, is an amazing driver—she really is! But she has one small challenge: sometimes, she forgets which way is left and which is right. There have been times when she's driving and I'm giving directions because I can't drive. I'll say, "*Babe, take a left here,*" and instead of turning left, she turns right. I'll say, "*Babe, I said left!*" And she'll respond, "*I am!*" But she's turned right instead.

Here's the thing: **our minds are the steering wheel of our lives**. You can't move in a new direction if you keep pointing toward the old one. So, where is the steering wheel of your life pointing?

Our minds are incredibly powerful. God gave us an extraordinary tool in our minds, and when our minds are connected to His Spirit, we can accomplish great things. But ultimately, your life will reflect your most dominant thoughts.

You can't reset your life while holding onto old thoughts. Let me ask you: *What are you thinking about? What's consuming your mind?* Think about what you're thinking about.

Let me take it further: **Your thoughts become actions. Your actions become habits. Your habits build your character, and your character shapes your destiny.** If you want to know where your life is headed, trace it back to your thoughts. Are you happy with the direction your life is going?

Negative thoughts will never lead to a positive life. If your mind is filled with negativity, it will impact every part of your life. For example, if you think you can't do something, you probably won't. If you believe you'll always be a victim, you'll likely continue living that way. If you think you can't overcome something, you never will. **Your thoughts have power!**

Too many of us are prisoners of our own minds instead of being drivers of our thoughts. But if you can change your thinking, you can change your life. **Change your thinking, and your life will follow**.

In Romans, Paul emphasizes the importance of mastering the mind. If anyone understood the battle of the mind, it was Paul. When you read some of his earlier writings, you might think he was all over the place—conflicted and confused. But that's good news for us because, let's be honest, we all feel a little crazy sometimes, right? Paul says at the end of Romans 7 (the passage that speaks about his struggle with sin), *"Praise be to God, through Jesus Christ our Lord!"*

Paul understood the struggle of the mind. Have you ever felt conflicted? Wanting to do the right thing but ending up doing the opposite? Maybe you've started a fast, but Krispy Kreme kept calling your name. Or you've tried to pray, but Instagram distracted you. It's a battle, right?

By the time we get to Romans 12, Paul urges us to *"be transformed by the renewing of your mind."* He understood that the mind is a powerful tool. Remember this: **Your life will always move in the direction of your strongest thoughts.** You can say one thing, but if your mind is thinking something else, your life will reflect your thoughts.

Paul grasped this concept well. He knew that the battle of the mind is critical. Here's what I'm telling you: **Most of life's battles are won or lost in the mind**. The question is, can you believe in your heart that God can renew your mind? In his letters to different churches, Paul consistently addressed the importance of mastering the mind.

Renewing the Mind

So, how do we begin to renew our minds? How can we reset our thinking? The first step is to **catch the lie**. Recognize the lie the enemy keeps feeding you. What's the thought that keeps dragging you down? What's the deception that tells you, *I can't do this* or *I'll never be good enough*? The enemy is always throwing lies our way, and too often, we take the bait. But every lie we believe adds another brick to the prison wall around our minds.

Just like with our phones, we must realize when something isn't working as it should. This could mean acknowledging emotional exhaustion, spiritual stagnation, or even a sense of disconnection from God. Being honest with yourself is crucial here. You can't reset what you're not willing to recognize. You think, *I'm not good enough*—there's another brick. *I'll always be a failure*—another brick. These lies build strongholds in our minds. But if you want to be free, you have to identify those lies. What's the one lie the enemy keeps whispering in your ear?

Paul writes in Ephesians 4:23-24, *"Let the Spirit renew your thoughts and attitudes."* Another translation says, *"Let the attitude of your mind be changed by the Spirit."* Paul is telling us to change the attitude of our minds and put on a new nature, created to be like God—truly righteous and holy. If you want to reset your life, it begins in your mind.

Next, **seek God intentionally**. When a phone is reset, it doesn't lose its connection to the network—it reconnects to the source. In the same way, we must reconnect to God. This is done through time spent in prayer, reading His Word, and inviting Him into your everyday moments. Make it a priority to sit still before God, even for just a few minutes a day. Ask Him to show you where you've gone off track and where He wants you to go.

Another key is to let go of the past. Just like when we back up our phones before resetting them, we must learn to release past hurts, failures, and even successes. We hold on to so many things that keep us stuck. Ask God to help you release anything that's hindering you from fully stepping into the new life He has for you.

Lastly, build new habits and routines that bring life. Resetting isn't a one-time thing—it's a continuous process. Surround yourself with people who will encourage and challenge you. Engage in meaningful activities that nurture your spiritual, emotional, and mental health. Join a small group, serve in a ministry, or find time to give back in some way. Keep doing what leads to life.

Practical steps to reset:

Pray intentionally: Start each day asking God for guidance.

Immerse in Scripture: Read a chapter a day or focus on a specific book that speaks to your current struggles.

Forgive and release: Write down things you need to let go of, and give them to God.

Make changes: Whether in your habits, your relationships, or your environment—adjust what's pulling you away from spiritual growth.

The beauty of God's grace is that we can always begin again. Just like resetting a phone, it clears out the clutter and brings us back to a fresh start with Him. This is where healing begins and where we rediscover the joy and purpose that comes with walking closely with our Creator.

Your Mind Shapes Your Life

Whatever enters your mind will eventually come out in your life. If you're constantly thinking critically, you'll develop a critical spirit. If you always think like a victim, you'll live with a victim mentality. Listen to me this morning: **If you want to change your life, you have to start with your mind**. Negative thoughts will never produce a positive life. What are you allowing into your mind?

Here's something important to know: every thought you have creates a neurochemical change in your brain. Studies show that when you think about something long enough, it literally rewires your brain. Some of us have been thinking the same way for so long that it's become a well-worn path in our brains. It's automatic now—when you're bored, you pick up your phone and scroll through Instagram because you've trained your mind to do that. When you're sad, you turn to emotional eating, because that's your go-to. **Your brain has created an easy path to follow**.

But here's the good news: **You can forge a new path**. You don't have to keep going down those old, destructive roads. Science calls it *rewiring the brain*; God calls it *renewing the mind*.

You are set apart because of Jesus Christ. You are being sanctified, and God is working in you through His Holy Spirit. The same Spirit that resurrected Jesus from the dead is resurrecting you every day, guiding you through the process of sanctification. You're not who you used to be, and thank God for that—you're on a journey, getting closer to Him every day.

Vultures and a Hummingbird

A vulture wakes up every day searching for dead things. You'll see them flying around, looking for what's lifeless along the road. Their focus is on finding death. But a hummingbird wakes up every day searching for sweet nectar. It travels to up to a thousand flowers just to find sweetness—it's looking for the good.

In the same way, **there are new mercies and new compassion waiting for you every morning**. If God is for you, who can be against you? It's time to stop looking for the dead things. You are not that failure. You are not that mistake. **God's grace is enough**. You can renew your mind.

Don't let the enemy hold you captive in his stronghold any longer. **In Jesus' name, you can demolish every stronghold!** You are new in Christ. You are not who you used to be, and your past doesn't define you. There is freedom in the name of Jesus!

The Briefing Room

Step Eight - Clean

Take one minute to clean your soul today. Meditate on God's Word, memorize God's Word, and move with God's Word. As you think and pray, you are pressing the reset button and cleaning out what was not from God. Every day, take a few moments to clean out the faithless thinking and reset with faith-filled thinking.

THE DECEPTION OF PRIDE

CHAPTER NINE

Back when Ronald Reagan was Governor of California, he gave a speech in Mexico City. As he spoke, he noticed the audience wasn't very responsive—there was little to no applause. After finishing his speech, Reagan sat down, bewildered and frustrated, thinking, *I gave a good speech; why didn't they respond?*

The next speaker came up, and the crowd erupted in applause. Not wanting to be the only one not clapping, Reagan joined in, clapping along with the crowd—despite not understanding a word, as the speaker was talking in Spanish. Suddenly, the ambassador sitting next to him leaned over and said, *"I don't think you want to do that."* Confused, Reagan asked why. The ambassador replied, *"He's interpreting your speech—you're clapping for yourself!"*

This story reflects the world we live in today. We live in a society where we're all clapping for ourselves, seeking validation and applause for our intelligence, looks, social media followers, and success.

If we're not clapping for ourselves, we're certainly seeking applause from others. Our culture is fixated on praise: *Did you see what I did today? Have you checked out my Instagram feed? Did you notice my accomplishments?* It's a constant craving for validation—*Clap for me!* At the center of this is the idol of self-pride.

Another illustration is the story of actress/singer Judy Garland, and it is one of great tragedy. If you are unfamiliar with

Judy Garland, she is the star of the classic film *The Wizard of Oz* and was the most famed star of her day. She had it all. Sadly, at the age of 47, her life ended. At the time of her death, the *New York Times* wrote an article that I think will resonate with many of us:

"LONDON, June 22—Judy Garland, whose successes on stage and screen were later overshadowed by the pathos of her personal life, was found dead in her home here today. Miss Garland's personal life often seemed a fruitless search for the happiness promised in 'Over the Rainbow,' the song she made famous in the movie *The Wizard of Oz.* Her father died when she was 12 years old; the pressures of adolescent stardom sent her to a psychiatrist at the age of 18; she was married five times; she was frequently ill; her singing voice faltered, and she suffered from the effects of drugs she once said were prescribed either to invigorate or tranquilize her. Judy Garland's career was marked by a compulsive quality that displayed itself even during her first performance at the age of 30 months at the New Grand Theater in Grand Rapids, Minn. Here, the story is told, she was singing 'Jingle Bells' at a Christmas program. She responded so favorably to the footlights that her father was forced to remove her after she repeated the song seven times! The other side of the compulsively vibrant, exhausting performances that were her stage hallmark was a seemingly unquenchable need for her audiences to respond with acclaim and affection. And often they did, screaming, 'We love you, Judy—we love you.'

Towards the end of her life, she was quoted as saying, 'In the silence of night I have often wished for just a few words of love from one man, rather than the applause of thousands of people.'

From Judy Garland's story, we recognize our own yearning to be accepted, our inclination to be applauded, and our desire just to be seen. This hunger can manifest itself in many ways. We crave attention from people because we never got it when we were young; the more compliments we receive, the happier we believe we can be; the more we please people, the better we feel about ourselves; we project onto people hoping to be noticed; if people applaud us for our work, then we'll be considered successful; we want to be valued; we want to have worth; we want to feel significant. Before we know it, we have become prisoners to people's opinions and to the idol of pride.

The Idol of Self

The glorification of "me." Look at what *I've* done, how brilliant *I* am, how much knowledge *I* have. While it's easy to point fingers at the world for this, the truth is, it's happening in the church as well. We can become intoxicated by our own anointing, positions, or gifts. We start drinking our own Kool-Aid, thinking we're smarter or more important than others.

One commentator noted that, in previous generations, people sought wisdom and knowledge from external sources. Today, we look inward and see ourselves as the ultimate authority. Augustine, one of the greatest Christian thinkers, said we are "curved inward on ourselves," instead of looking outward toward God.

We rely on our own thoughts: *What do I think about this? What's my plan? What's my heart telling me to do?* Instead of seeking God's direction, we trust in ourselves. This is where pride takes over. Self-reliance sits on the throne of our hearts, and we believe we know best.

The Bible warns us about this in 2 Timothy, where it says that in the last days, people will become "lovers of themselves." This is a serious issue. The problem with making ourselves the god of our lives is that the "god of me" is limited by the flaws within me. If I'm the god of my life, I'm bound by my own weaknesses and shortcomings. **Pride blinds us to our own limitations**. We forget that we don't have all the knowledge, wisdom, or strength we need.

The "god of me" doesn't want to listen to the wisdom of God or others. It resists correction. This is a major problem today—*I don't need anyone telling me what to do. I know what I'm doing.* We want to be in control and make our own decisions: *I'll date who I want, marry who I want, spend my money how I want, and worship when and how I want. Don't tell me how to raise my kids or treat my spouse. I've got this figured out.*

But when we place ourselves on the throne of our hearts, we're headed for destruction. We drown in the consequences of the "god of me" because it is not as wise, strong, or capable as we think. There's only one God who knows all, who holds all wisdom and power. It's time to remove ourselves from the throne and put God back where He belongs.

Is God on the throne of your heart today, or are you in charge? It's time to remove the idol of self. Maybe you shouldn't be making all the decisions in your life. Maybe it's time to lean into God and allow Him to guide you. God, You make the choices. Lead me in my relationships, my marriage, my family, *and* my finances. Help me in every area of my life.

Here's something important to understand: God will not share the throne of your heart. You can't live life however you want and expect God to fit in beside you. God doesn't want to rent a room in your heart—He wants to own it. There's a huge difference between renting and owning.

And here's the beautiful part: God desires to lead your life out of His deep, eternal love for you. He says, *"If you let Me take the driver's seat of your life, I'll steer you in the right direction. I'll lead you to a good future, a destiny filled with hope."* God has blessings and promises for your life, but you need to let Him drive. Otherwise, you're going to crash and burn. He will take you to the promised land, but you need to give Him control.

If you can empty yourself of pride, you can be filled with the Holy Spirit. If you want the Holy Spirit to take over your life today, say, *"Less of me, and more of You, God. Take me off the throne, and You sit on the throne of my heart"*

The war of the soul can be won through the word of the Lord. My prayer is that by now you have read, seen, and understand that your soul is of ultimate value. You are loved by Almighty God. But as long as you and I ignore the battle plan God has left for us and follow our own thoughts, ideas, and selfish will, we cannot experience ultimate victory. This powerful idol, the idol of self, has to be defeated so that you and I can begin to heal and live fully.

We all struggle with idols, and while they may not look like the idols of ancient times, our culture is full of modern idols. But what is an idol?

An idol is anything we value above God. As Pastor John Piper put it: *"Anything in the world that successfully competes with our love for God is an idol."* Anything that competes for your attention, time, or worship can become an idol. This means relationships, people, and even material things can become idols in our lives.

Today, one of the biggest idols we face is our iPhones. Think about it—how often do we give more attention to our phones than we give to God? The first thing we do when we wake up is check our emails, texts, or social media, instead of giving the first moments of the day to God by saying, *"Lord, I worship You. I love You. Thank You."* We have so many idols—people, places, products, and even ourselves. Pride, self-image—these things can easily become idols.

The Psalmist writes about the idols of humanity and their inability to help us in Psalm 115:2-8 - *"Why should the nations say, 'Where is their God?' Our God is in the heavens; He does all that He pleases. Their idols are silver and gold, the work of human hands. They have mouths, but do not speak; eyes, but do not see. They have ears, but do not hear; noses, but do not smell. They have hands, but do not feel; feet, but do not walk; and they do not make a sound in their throat. Those who make them become like them; so do all who trust in them."* (Psalm 115:2-8)

John Calvin once said, *"The human heart is a perpetual factory of idols."* Think about that. Our hearts are constantly producing idols. Every day, something is vying for your attention, for your devotion, trying to take God's place. Something is always calling for you to worship it, to give it your time, energy, and value above God. So the question is, **What idol is sitting on the throne of my heart today?** Is it my phone? My relationships? How people validate me? My career or position in life?

Our hearts are continually creating idols. We must ask God to be the only one sitting on the throne of our hearts. Humanity has a long history of idol worship, and we must be cautious.

This is how Satan first tempted humanity. In Genesis 3:5, the serpent said to Eve, *"For God knows that when you eat from it, your eyes will be opened, and you will be like God, knowing good and evil."* Notice how Satan played on the idol of pride. He tempted Eve by suggesting that she could *"be like God."* Today, humanity still struggles with that same desire—to be like God.

We see it in how we handle morality. *"Let's see what Scripture says about sex."* But many respond, *"No, I know better than God."* We see it in conversations about gender, anger, or behavior—*"I know what's best. I don't need God telling me what to do."*

We've removed God from the throne of our hearts and placed ourselves there. This has deep implications for our culture and society. We were created to worship, and when we remove God from His rightful place, we naturally end up worshipping something else.

Maybe you're thinking, *"I don't worship anything, not even God."* But even atheists worship something. **Worship** means to give worth to something, to declare it valuable. When you invest your time and energy into something or someone, you are worshipping it. If that thing takes precedence over God, it becomes an idol.

In Exodus 32, when Moses led the Israelites out of Egypt, they found themselves waiting in the desert while Moses went up Mount Sinai to meet with God. When Moses took longer than expected, the people grew impatient. In their impatience, they created a golden calf to worship, melting down their jewelry to form an idol. Their hearts were made to worship something, and when God seemed to take too long, they returned to the idols they had known in Egypt.

When God doesn't respond as quickly as we'd like, we often revert to old habits, old ways of thinking, and former idols. We tell ourselves, *"God, You're taking too long, so I'll take control. I'll make my own decisions."* But that leads to destruction.

In Exodus 32, because of their sin in creating the golden calf, 3,000 people died. But in Acts 2, when the disciples waited on the Lord, the Holy Spirit came down, and 3,000 people were saved. If we can wait on God and worship Him instead of rushing into our own solutions, He will fill us, guide us, and lead us. But if we chase after the "golden calves" in our lives, we will end up destroyed.

The Danger of Pride

Look at the last 30 or 40 years, and you'll see Pride is a secret sin. It blinds us. We are all drawn toward idols, and pride is one of the most dangerous. When we turn away from God and allow idols to take His place in our lives, we lose our way.

We must be aware of the idols we allow to creep into our hearts. Whether it's pride, our phones, relationships, or anything else that distracts us from God, we need to remove it from the throne and allow God to take His rightful place. He alone is worthy of our worship.

We all have feelings, inclinations, and desires, but we must learn to align those with God's will. **Don't follow your feelings—follow God**. The that self-worship has led to pain, broken relationships, and turmoil.

Unfortunately, in today's world, many are no longer serving the God of Abraham, Isaac, and Jacob. Instead, they're serving the god of "me, myself, and I." We make choices based not on God's guidance, but on how we feel. That's why we end up in trouble—in our families, marriages, and relationships—not because God led us to make those choices, but because we followed our own desires.

Pride is a deceiver. We say, "*I'm not going to serve. I'm not going to connect. I'm not going to fix this issue or apologize.*" The god of self tells us we know best, but self is a liar, and pride is a deceiver.

The Protestant reformer Martin Luther once said, "*Whatever your heart clings to and relies upon, that is your God.*" You can choose to trust in God, or you can trust in yourself. If you trust in God, He will lead you. But if you trust in yourself and your feelings, you won't get very far.

We need to honestly examine ourselves. If we're truly honest, we'll see that we're not as great as we think we are. And I know that may not sound encouraging, but it's necessary. Our culture promotes the idea of being "self-made," but the reality is, we aren't self-made. If we were, we'd be able to remake ourselves whenever we wanted—but we can't.

There's a God who made us, and without Him, we are limited in what we can do. Yes, God has given us talents and gifts, and many of us are incredibly skilled. But deep down, we're all sinners in need of God. If we're honest, we know that we need Him. The Bible says in Psalm 14:2-3, "*The Lord looks down from heaven on the children of men to see if there are any who understand, who seek after God. They have all turned aside; together they have become corrupt. There is none who does good, not even one."*

Wow. That's the human heart—corrupt and sinful. No matter how kind, nice, or gifted you are, if you place that corrupt heart on the throne of your life, it will lead you to destruction. Yes, you're gifted and talented, and God wants to use those gifts for His glory. But make sure **He's** the one sitting on the throne of your heart because, deep down, the heart is deceitful and wicked. The Bible says, "*Who can understand the heart?"* (Jeremiah 17:9). So first, we must look inside ourselves.

Look Outside

What does it mean to seek outside ourselves? It means recognizing God's power in creation. We can look around at the world He created and realize that there is something far greater than ourselves. I may think I'm talented or smart, but when I look at the clouds, the trees, the rainbow in the sky, and the shining sun, I see evidence of a God who is much wiser, stronger, and more powerful than I am. The intricate beauty and design of creation remind me that **I need God** to lead my life, not myself. He's the one who is mighty, intelligent, and capable.

Romans 1:20-23 says, "*For since the creation of the world God's invisible qualities—His eternal power and divine nature—have been clearly seen, being understood from what has been made, so that people are without excuse. For although they knew God, they neither glorified Him as God nor gave thanks to Him, but their thinking became futile and their foolish hearts were darkened. Although they claimed to be wise, they became fools and exchanged the glory of the immortal God for images made to look like a mortal human being and birds and animals and reptiles.*"

Paul tells us that we have no excuse. By looking at creation, we can clearly see that there is a mighty and good God who is worthy of praise. He's the Creator of everything, and just as He formed the universe, He wants to shape and guide our lives. But too often, we exchange the glory of God for our own foolish pride or something that resembles us.

How many times have we bowed down to ourselves in our decisions and choices? We may not physically bow to a statue, but we often worship our own desires and pride. We need to stop looking inward for answers and start seeking God.

Where does help come from? Psalm 121:2 reminds us: "*My help comes from the Lord, the Maker of heaven and earth."*Today, we need to stop bowing down to ourselves and begin to bow down before God. We need to acknowledge that we aren't that great on our own. We've been bowing to our own decisions, plans, emotions, and feelings for too long. But today, let's humble ourselves before God and receive His help.

In Acts 1:8, Jesus told His disciples, "*But you will receive power when the Holy Spirit comes upon you; and you will be My witnesses in Jerusalem, and in all Judea and Samaria, and to the ends of the earth."* After Jesus ascended to heaven, the disciples went to the upper room and waited. In Acts 2, the Holy Spirit came down upon them, and they began to speak in tongues, prophesy, and praise God. It was a powerful moment.

The Power of Humility

Some of us have been intoxicated by our own pride—we've "drunk our own Kool-Aid." But it's time to humble ourselves. And here's the good news: when we realize there's a battle against pride and we intentionally choose humility, we step into one of the most powerful promises in all of the Bible: "*Humble yourselves before the Lord, and He will lift you up*" (James 4:10). God isn't looking to humiliate us; through humility, we unlock the most profound blessings possible. We must wage war on our pride.

The Briefing Room

Step Nine - Concede

Take one minute to observe and analyze where pride might be lurking in your life. Have you blocked out voices of concern or advice in your life? One of the best weapons you will have in this war for your soul is friends of the soul. Drop the pride and ask for advice today to continue to win the battle over the soul.

DON'T SETTLE THERE

CHAPTER TEN

The Perseverance of Lincoln

In 1809, a man was born who faced tremendous challenges in the first 50 years of his life. By the age of nine, he lost his mother, a devastating blow. At 21, the business he worked for went bankrupt, leaving him without a job. At 26, he lost his fiancée to illness. At 27, he suffered from nervous breakdowns. Failure after failure seemed to follow him.

Undeterred, he entered politics but lost his congressional races at 36 and 37. Yet, despite all these setbacks, he didn't give up. At the age of 51, he became the 16th president of the United States—**Abraham Lincoln**. His life is a testimony to perseverance and refusal to settle in the midst of adversity.

Like Lincoln, many successful people could have given up when life got tough. Michael Jordan was cut from his high school basketball team during his sophomore year. Oprah Winfrey was fired from her local news station because she didn't "fit in." But they didn't settle for failure—they pushed forward.

Thomas Edison once said that he found 10,000 ways an invention wouldn't work before he finally succeeded. And Albert Einstein didn't speak until he was four years old—some thought he was slow. Today, his name is synonymous with genius. These stories show what happens when people refuse to settle and choose to press on through obstacles and challenges, determined not to stop until they reach their goal.

It's not what happens to us that defines us, but how we navigate those challenges. The human tendency is to settle when life gets tough. When obstacles pile up and everything seems to be going wrong, it's easier to quit, throw in the towel, and say, *"I'm done."* It's much easier to stop when your courage is gone, when you're worn out, and when those difficult texts and phone calls seem never-ending. In those moments, it's tempting to think, *"I'm okay with where I'm at. I'll just settle here."*

Stretch Beyond Settling

But here's the dilemma: **it's always easier to settle than it is to stretch**. Settling is far easier than pushing yourself beyond your comfort zone. It's easier to settle for disappointments than to stretch for your dreams. It's easier to settle in your faith than to stretch and believe that God can do more. It's easier to stay stuck in the past than to stretch forward into a wide-open future.

Settling is always easier. But here's the question for you today: **Have you settled in an area of your life?** Have you settled for mediocrity? Maybe you've settled for an average marriage—*"At least we're getting along, right?"* Or maybe you've settled for an average relationship with your kids, thinking, *"It's okay; at least we're together."*

Have you settled in brokenness, accepting it as your identity? *"I guess I'm always going to be broken. I guess I'll always be addicted. I'm just the black sheep of the family."* Over time, where we settle becomes our identity. We start to believe we are defined by our circumstances: *"I'm the broken one, I'm the sick one, I'm the messed-up one in my family."* We carry that label around because it's what people have always said about us.

But when we settle in defeat, we also allow generational patterns of brokenness to continue. Instead of saying, *"I'm going to stretch and believe that God can do something new!"* we stay stuck. We serve a God who can do the impossible, yet we often settle for average when we could be stretching for something greater.

You don't have to stay stuck in addiction, brokenness, or despair. God has something better for you, but it requires stretching. It's time to stretch your faith, stretch your expectations, and stretch beyond the limits you've placed on yourself. Don't settle for less when you serve a **God of more**.

It's easier to settle than to stretch toward God's extraordinary plans. But we cannot afford to settle for mediocrity. We must stretch and believe God for bigger things. We must continue to move forward in faith.

Here's the reality: When you stop wandering in the pain of the past, you start enjoying the wonder of God's promises. It's time to cut off the past. Yes, we've all lost something, we've all faced hardship. But don't settle in your past. **Move forward into the future.**

Charles Spurgeon once said, *"The Lord picks His best soldiers out of the highlands of affliction."* So if you're going through something tough, know that God is preparing you for what's to come. You're not meant to settle there.

Get Out of Ur

In Genesis, God chose a man—Abraham—and through him, He formed a nation. When you step back and look at the bigger picture, you see that God was showing humanity what their lives, families, and even nations could look like if they chose to live, love, and honor Him. God chose a specific people, who would become the nation of Israel, to demonstrate His blessings and goodness to the world.

God intended to bless Israel so that others would see the benefits of serving and honoring Him, rather than wasting time worshipping false idols. Throughout Genesis, God separates His people, making them holy and demonstrating to the world what happens when a nation honors and loves Him.

"Now these are the generations of Terah. Terah fathered Abram, Nahor, and Haran; and Haran fathered Lot. Haran died in

the presence of his father Terah in the land of his birth, in Ur of the Chaldeans. And Abram and Nahor took wives. The name of Abram's wife was Sarai, and the name of Nahor's wife, Milcah, the daughter of Haran, the father of Milcah and Iscah. Now Sarai was barren; she had no child. Terah took Abram his son and Lot the son of Haran, his grandson, and Sarai his daughter-in-law, his son Abram's wife, and they went forth together from Ur of the Chaldeans to go into the land of Canaan. But when they came to Haran, they settled there." (Genesis 11:27-31)

Notice that last part: "*But when they came to Haran, they settled there."* Let's focus on the phrase: "**They settled there."**

God called Abraham, who was living in a place called **Ur of the Chaldeans**. For some of us today, *Ur* represents the place where we've been stuck for too long. Ur of the Chaldeans is modern-day Iraq, and God called Abraham out of that land to lead him to Canaan, which is modern-day Israel. God had a beautiful promise for Abraham in Canaan, a land described as *"flowing with milk and honey,"* a place of abundance and blessing. Yet, many of us are still stuck in our own personal "Ur," unable to step into the promises of God.

Ur was a place full of idolatry and false worship. If you study ancient times, you'll find that Abraham's homeland was filled with idol worship. God called Abraham out of a land of confusion and disbelief and into a land of direction, promise, future, and hope. The people of Ur, including Abraham's own father, Terah, were idol worshipers. According to Jewish tradition, Terah was even an idol manufacturer, and the primary god they worshiped was the moon god. In fact, Sarah, Abraham's wife, had a name that originally meant "queen of the universe," a title connected to the moon goddess they revered.

But God called Abraham out of that confusion. He called him out of a life focused on false gods and into a future filled with promise. We serve a God who calls us **out of our messes**, out of our brokenness, and into His plans for a greater future. As we begin this year, I believe God is calling many of us out of our own personal "Ur"—out of toxic relationships, out of addictions, out of confusion. **God has something much greater in store for you!**

God has a hope and a future for each of us. He's a good God who calls us forward into His promises. He speaks to us gently through the Holy Spirit, and some of you can already feel His prompting as you read this. Maybe you know there are phone numbers you need to delete, websites you need to block, or unhealthy relationships you need to end. As sweet and tempting as those things may seem, God is calling you out of them and into something far better. **Don't settle!**

God always calls us into something greater. He called Abraham out of confusion and idolatry. And what I love about Abraham is that, despite the noise and distractions around him, he had an ear to hear God's voice. One of the most important lessons we can learn from Abraham's life is this: **listen for direction.**

Can you hear me Now?

Here's a question I've been reflecting on: *Is God trying to speak to me, but I'm not listening?* Many of us are great at talking to God. We pray daily, talk to Him on our way to work, on our way home, and throughout the day. But how often do we stop to listen? Too often, we come to God with a list of things we want, but we don't take the time to hear what **He** wants to say.

God, I love You, but sometimes my prayers can be a bit dramatic. I've prayed things like, *"God, strike them with something—maybe not something too bad, but something like a stomachache or their face breaking out,"* Or when I'm stuck in traffic, *"God, can You please do something about this traffic?"* We tend to approach God with our list of needs: *"God, I need healing, I need provision. Could You just make my paycheck a little thicker this week?"* But we need to remember that God is not a genie or an ATM machine. He provides wisdom and guidance, and we are called to serve and honor Him.

The real question is, **are we listening?** I wonder if God has been trying to speak to us, but we haven't created the space to truly hear Him. We need Him in our marriages, our families, raising kids, making business decisions, navigating relationships, and every other area of life. If we are going to win the battles for the soul we need an open ear and a faithful heart to follow the path.

To move forward in life, we need direction. Abraham was surrounded by idolatry—his father, family, and the people around him worshipped false gods. Yet, when God called Abraham, he listened. **Do you have an ear to hear what God wants to tell you?**

Hebrews 12:1 says, "*Therefore, since we are surrounded by so great a cloud of witnesses, let us also lay aside every weight and sin which clings so closely, and let us run with endurance the race that is set before us."* We can't run the race God has for us if we're weighed down by distractions. Today, we need to lay aside those distractions.

If we continue reading in Genesis 11, we see that Terah, Abraham's father, passed away. But in Genesis 12, the focus shifts back to Abraham. At first glance, this seems like a chronological progression, but it's actually the Hebrew way of storytelling—providing background before diving into the main narrative. Genesis 12:1 says, "*Now the Lord said to Abram, 'Go from your country and your kindred and your father's house to the land that I will show you.'*"

If we aren't careful, we might think God called Abraham after his father died. But in the book of Acts, Stephen clarifies that God actually called Abraham while he was still in Mesopotamia, before they even reached Haran. Acts 7:2-3 says, "*The God of glory appeared to our father Abraham when he was in Mesopotamia, before he lived in Haran, and said to him, 'Go out from your land and from your kindred and go into the land that I will show you.'*"

So, what happened? God called Abraham out of Ur of the Chaldeans, and along the way to Canaan, they stopped in Haran, a city halfway to the promised land. Genesis 11 tells us that they *settled* in Haran. Terah, Abraham's father, likely suggested they rest for a few days, but those days turned into years. Haran was comfortable, so they began to settle there—opening businesses and building a life.

But here's the thing: **some of us have also settled at the halfway point in life.** You've settled in your *Haran*, in the middle of your promises, goals, and dreams. You've written down visions that God has given you, yet you've stopped halfway. Haran wasn't meant to be their final destination; **Canaan was.** God is saying, "*I want you to move forward. There's more for you.*"

Interestingly, Haran was also the name of Terah's first son, who had died earlier. While scholars believe the city wasn't connected to the son, we can't ignore the emotional weight this may have had on Terah. Perhaps when Terah arrived in Haran, he thought, "*This is too painful. This reminds me of the loss I've faced,*" and decided to settle there. The city may have become a symbol of his grief, causing him to stop moving forward.

Many of us today are sitting in a place of pain, stuck because life has been hard. We've experienced struggles and tears, and instead of moving forward, we've settled in that place of difficulty. We've accepted it as our identity—*brokenness, rejection, loneliness*—when God has so much more in store for us. You've settled in your calling and allowed pain to hold you captive.

But God is calling you today: **don't settle there.** That's not your final destination. I know it's been painful, but that place of hurt is not where you're meant to stay. Yes, you've experienced loss, but that doesn't mean you're supposed to stop moving forward. **Keep pushing through.**

Abraham could have settled too. He lost his brother just as his father had, but instead of stopping, Abraham believed God, and it was counted to him as righteousness. He continued moving toward Canaan because he knew **Haran wasn't the final destination**. He might have paused, but he didn't settle permanently—he persevered through difficulties.

Perseverance of a Snail

Imagine if Abraham had settled in Haran. The Bible is full of examples of people who didn't settle because they trusted God's promises. Paul says in Philippians 3:13-14, "*Forgetting what lies behind and straining forward to what lies ahead, I press on toward the goal for the prize of the upward call of God in Christ Jesus.*" What if Paul had settled when things got hard? What if Abraham Lincoln had given up after losing his first election? What if Thomas Edison had stopped after his early failures?

Your soul might have been trapped in the many deceptions we've covered so far. The past might have been bad, but there is a wide open future for you and me. Do not buy into the false mirages of this world and settle in Haran. You can keep going to the greener and greater areas of life that God has for you. It was Charles Spurgeon, the English preacher, who said, "By perseverance, the snail reached the ark."

I love that statement. Life is not a sprint but a marathon. Your soul is loved, and although war may be waging against us, greater is He who is with us (1 John 4:4). You can get up again and again and again and move forward into all God has for you.

As you read this, I know God is prompting you to move forward—**and I know you can feel it too.** God is telling you to move on. You know what needs to be left behind—certain attitudes, mindsets, relationships, or places that no longer serve you. God is calling you out of your *Haran*.

Some of you have endured pain, heartache, and brokenness over the last few years. God knows what you've been through, but He's using those challenges and adversities to shape you. **You're not meant to stop there.**

God is making you stronger, shaping you into a soldier, a man or a woman of God through these trials. But **don't settle**—He has so much more for you.

The Briefing Room

Step Ten - Correct

Take one minute to correct your path today. Perhaps you were thinking that your life would never change, it didn't matter, or your choices weren't important, but that is the furthest thing from the truth. Your decisions matter. Continue to correct your thinking into godly, biblical thinking. Don't stop now; correct your path and continue your steps.

MOVING FORWARD

CHAPTER ELEVEN

I recently read about a man named R.U. Darby, who lived during the late 1800s. Darby heard about the gold rush happening on the West Coast and, eager for opportunity, invested thousands of dollars in mining equipment. He gathered his uncle, and together they headed out west in search of gold.

After arriving, they began mining and quickly found a gold vein. Excited, they thought they had struck it rich. But after just a few days, the vein ran dry. Frustrated, Darby believed all the gold was gone and quickly gave up hope. Discouraged, he sold all his expensive equipment to a local man for just a few hundred dollars, boarded a train, and returned home.

Here's the twist: the man who bought Darby's equipment decided to keep digging. Just **three feet** from where Darby had stopped, the man found one of the richest veins of gold in California. He became a multi-millionaire, while Darby became known as the man who quit too soon—**just three feet from gold**.

When I heard that story, I couldn't help but think about our walk with God. How many of us have stopped just three feet away from a miracle? How many times have we stopped believing for a breakthrough, healing, or the promises God has for our lives? Maybe we gave up praying, thinking God would never come through. Perhaps, like Darby, we quit just before God was about to perform the miracle we needed.

I wonder if there are areas in your life where you've stopped believing. Areas where your faith was once strong, but now it's running low. Maybe you've come today lacking the fervor and spirit you once had when you believed God could do all things.

Are you quitting too soon? Are you giving up right before God is about to bring the breakthrough?

Many times, we quit because we don't truly believe God will keep His promises. We might pray, sing, and worship, but deep down, we doubt that He will do what He said. We start treating God like people in our lives who may break their promises or let us down.

Here's the truth: **God is not like that**. He is faithful to His word. What He has promised, He will fulfill. God never abandons His children or leaves us without hope. So today, let's decide not to quit too soon. Let's keep moving forward in faith, trusting that God is with us, that He is for us, and that He will bring to pass everything He has promised.

Unbelief the Thief

Sometimes, we stop trusting God because we wonder if He will actually do what He promised. We might think God has somehow misled us or won't come through. So, we quit. We stop obeying, and we don't move forward in life because we doubt His faithfulness. But the truth is this: **our disobedience often stems from distrust**.

We may not trust God enough to step out in faith, to believe He can save our loved ones or deliver us from addiction. We think our situation is too far gone. We hesitate to take that leap of faith because we're afraid we might look foolish if God doesn't come through.

The real issue is that unbelief robs us of vision. As we move forward, I believe God wants to raise up people full of vision and faith. People who say, *"I believe God can turn my family, my life, and my situation around."* But when unbelief takes root in our hearts, it clouds our vision, robbing us of the ability to see what God can do in the next year, the next month, or even tomorrow.

Unbelief allows the lies of the enemy to play on repeat in our minds, telling us we'll never be leaders, that we'll never make an impact. And before we know it, we've stopped dreaming and stopped believing. We've given up, **just three feet from a miracle**. But let me remind you: **God often thrives in the most challenging moments of life**.

Think about it:

It wasn't until Daniel was in the lion's den that God sent an angel to shut the lions 'mouths.

It wasn't until David stood before Goliath that God gave him the strength to defeat the giant.

It wasn't until Paul was shackled in prison that God gave him the courage to keep preaching.

It wasn't until Moses stood at the edge of the Red Sea that God parted the waters.

And it wasn't until Jesus lay in the tomb that the Spirit of God breathed life back into Him, raising Him from the dead.

So, even if your life feels like it's hit a dead end, remember that it's often in those moments that God is positioning you for a miracle. **He specializes in doing the impossible!** God can do exceedingly, abundantly, above all we ask or imagine. Are you thankful for a God like that?

Maybe you feel stuck, but I'm writing this to stir up your faith. You might be on the edge of giving up, but God is just getting started. You have to keep moving forward. I believe in a God who can do more than we can ask or think, and I want to encourage you today: **don't quit too soon**.

Norman Vincent Peale once said, "*It's always too soon to quit.*" Vince Lombardi echoed this with, "*Winners never quit.*" And the Apostle Paul reminds us, "*Let us not grow weary in doing good, for in due season we will reap a harvest if we do not give up.*"

Even Jesus said, "*Anyone who puts their hand to the plow and looks back is not fit for the kingdom of God.*"

So, I ask you this: **are you three feet from your miracle?** Don't give up now. God has more for you! Keep believing. Don't stop. God is able, and you are reading this book for a reason. In just a moment, He can turn your situation around, break chains, heal the sick, and raise the dead. **He is able!**

A heart full of faith can overcome any giant. If you hold onto your faith, you can face impossibilities. You may be up against a giant, but God is on your side, and He will help you overcome it.

Numbers 14:1-9 says:

"That night, all the members of the community raised their voices and wept aloud. All the Israelites grumbled against Moses and Aaron, and the whole assembly said to them, 'If only we had died in Egypt or in this wilderness! Why is the Lord bringing us to this land only to let us fall by the sword? Our wives and children will be taken as plunder. Wouldn't it be better for us to go back to Egypt?' And they said to each other, 'We should choose a leader and go back to Egypt.' Moses and Aaron fell face down in front of the whole Israelite assembly. Joshua son of Nun and Caleb son of Jephunneh, who were among those who had explored the land, tore their clothes and said to the entire Israelite assembly, 'The land we

passed through and explored is exceedingly good. If the Lord is pleased with us, He will lead us into that land, a land flowing with milk and honey, and will give it to us. Only do not rebel against the Lord. And do not be afraid of the people of the land, because we will devour them. Their protection is gone, but the Lord is with us. Do not be afraid of them.'"

This story is full of drama and faith. The people of God were finally free from Egypt, standing on the brink of the Promised Land. God had called Abraham out of Ur, the land of the Chaldeans, and promised him a land flowing with milk and honey. But Abraham, just like many of us, initially settled halfway. God told him, "*This is not the land I have for you—get up and keep moving.*" God's direction is always forward.

Keep on Moving

If you feel stuck today, let me tell you: **God wants you to move forward**. He called Abraham, and after generations of ups and downs, the people of Israel found themselves oppressed in Egypt for over 400 years. But God delivered them, and they stood on the verge of entering the land He had promised to their forefather, Abraham.

The Israelites had grown as a people and a nation, but they remained enslaved until the day Moses, their deliverer, arrived. You know the story—whether from the Bible or maybe even from *The Prince of Egypt*. Moses confronts Pharaoh and says, *"Let my people go!"* After a series of plagues, Pharaoh finally relents, and 2 million Israelites leave Egypt, heading toward the Promised Land.

As they marched out of Egypt, they looked back and saw the Egyptian army pursuing them. It's easy to trust God when there are no threats, but the real test comes when enemies are after you, fear is whispering lies, and anxiety is telling you that you will never move forward. Winning the war sometimes comes down to beating that anxiety.

Despite the threats, God opened the Red Sea, allowing the Israelites to cross safely. Once they reached the other side, God closed the sea over the Egyptian army, drowning them. **I love that God fights our battles for us**. They crossed over, but soon they were at the Jordan River. You would think that after witnessing the miracle at the Red Sea, they would have faith that God could help them cross the Jordan too.

But in Numbers 14, we see a different story unfold. They were just *three feet* from the Promised Land, yet they were filled with doubt and fear. Despite having seen the Red Sea part—walking through walls of water, a sight like no other—they stood in front of the Jordan River and lost their faith.

Moses sent twelve spies into the land to explore it. After forty days, the spies returned with mixed reports. Yes, the land was good—overflowing with milk, honey, and massive clusters of grapes. But they were afraid of the giants who lived there—fearsome, ugly giants with extra toes and eyes like monsters, descendants of Goliath's kin. The spies also mentioned fortified cities and evil kings. Their conclusion? "*We won't be able to take the land."*

Because of the bad report from ten of the spies, **2 million people were infected with unbelief** and chose not to move forward. This raises an important question: **who is in your circle?** Whose voices are you allowing to influence your life? Here's a powerful truth - Grasshopper mindset hold you back from giant like faith"

Choice of Voices

Be cautious of the negative voices around you. The enemy will whisper lies during worship, reminding you of your past and discouraging you from raising your hands in praise. These faithless voices tell you that you can't serve God, can't restore your marriage, can't change your family's future. That's why it's crucial to surround yourself with people full of faith.

Joshua and Caleb stood firm, despite the negative reports. They acknowledged the challenges—yes, there were giants and fortified cities—but they declared, *"If God promised it, He will do it."* We all need a Joshua and Caleb in our lives—people who, when our faith is wavering, will stand up and boldly declare, *"God will fulfill His promise!"*

Joshua and Caleb were full of faith. Even when the odds seemed insurmountable, they believed God could deliver on His promises. They weren't in denial about the difficulties ahead, but they trusted in God's power. I believe there are some "Joshua and Caleb" people reading this book—people who believe that God has a vision for their church, their city, and for the impossible situations in their lives.

We need people of faith who say, *"Yes, the giants are real, but God is bigger!"* We need voices in our lives that speak hope, not negativity. God is able to do exceedingly, abundantly more than we can ever imagine. We need people who remind us of that truth and believe with us for healing, restoration, and salvation.

Faith and fear are contagious. The people we surround ourselves with can either infect us with fear or inspire us with faith. Have you noticed that when you're around people full of fear, it's easy to adopt that fear? They say things like, *"There are giants in the land,"* and suddenly, you start believing it too. But when you're around people full of faith, they remind you that if God made one church grow, He can fill up another. If He restored one marriage, He can restore yours. If He healed someone, He can heal you. Both fear and faith are contagious.

Look at what happened with the Israelites. Because of the disbelief of ten spies, 2 million people spent **40 years wandering in the desert**. They were just three feet from their miracle and chose to turn back instead of moving forward. **Don't quit three feet from your miracle.**

There's a fundamental difference between the Moses generation and the Joshua generation. The Moses generation needed to see miracles to believe, but 40 years later, Joshua led a new generation who believed first and then saw the miracles. The Moses generation saw the Promised Land, but the Joshua generation walked in it. The Moses generation dreamed about it but gave up too soon, while the Joshua generation conquered it.

You are called to conquer. We're no longer part of the Moses generation—we belong to the Joshua generation. Joshua, in the Old Testament, is a type of Christ—a foreshadowing of Jesus. In fact, the name Joshua in Greek is the same as Jesus. Just as Joshua led the Israelites into the Promised Land, Jesus leads us into every promise God has for us.

What Joshua did physically—helping the Israelites cross into the Promised Land—**Jesus does spiritually**, leading us from death to life, from darkness to light. We serve under the Jesus generation, where every promise is *"Yes and Amen."* I don't know about you, but I'm thankful that Jesus went to the cross and defeated the grave so that we wouldn't have to stay stuck but could move forward into everything He has for us.

Today can be the day of new beginnings for you and I. Where we start to hear the war and heal the soul. Where we begin to close the door on all the distractions trying to weigh down the soul, and open our eyes to all the possibilities God has for us. Where we choose to live above the average mundane life that the enemy of the soul wants us to accept, and keep moving forward to everything God has planned for us. Receive the healing for your soul, as you get up to fight and move forward.

Giants Fall Too

Wake up every morning and **believe the promises of God**. We are called believers, yet too often we don't fully live out what it means to believe. If God said it, He will do it. Sometimes, we need to preach to ourselves—look in the mirror and declare, *"I am a child of God. I am called. I am redeemed. I am adopted. God's promises for me are true."* Hebrews 11:6 says, *"Without faith, it is impossible to please God, because anyone who comes to Him must believe that He exists and that He rewards those who earnestly seek Him."*

It's time to remind ourselves of His promises and live by faith. We are called to trust that **every promise in His Word** is for us, and God is faithful to fulfill it. Also advance through every open door of opportunity. God wants you to **move forward,** to advance into all that He has for your life. Don't stay stuck in fear or doubt. Some of us are just *three feet* from the promise, three feet from the miracle, and fear is holding us back. God wants to loose those chains and set us free to move forward.

How many times have we asked God to open doors for us, only to hesitate when He does? We see the opportunity but don't walk through it. It's time to **step out in faith** and advance into the future God has prepared for us. Don't let fear keep you from walking through the doors that God has opened. **Move forward with boldness.**

Joshua and the Israelites didn't just see the Promised Land—they walked into it and conquered it. **You are called to conquer,** not just to dream. You are called to **walk in the promises of God,** not just think about them. Jesus has already made a way for us to step into our calling and purpose.

It's time to stop holding back and **walk boldly** into all that God has for you. Too many of us dream but never take action. Now is the time to move from dreaming to doing. Ephesians 2:10 says, "*For we are His workmanship, created in Christ Jesus for good works, which God prepared beforehand that we should walk in them.*" Not wait, not stop, but **walk** in what He has called us to.

Today, someone needs to take a step forward. Don't just wait for the perfect moment—**walk forward in faith** and step into your calling.

We believe, we advance, and we **conquer**. Pause for a moment and say a prayer of victory: **You are going to conquer every giant**. Yes, there may be giants in front of you, but Romans 8 reminds us that **we are more than conquerors through Christ Jesus**. We are on the winning team! This war has already been won, now we need to walk it our in our everyday battles. There is a war, but we have already won!

What can separate us from the love of Christ? Nothing—no stress, no hardship, no principality. **Nothing** will be able to separate us from the love of Christ, who has called us to be more than conquerors. This, my friend, is what it means to be more than a conqueror—because **if God is for you, nothing can stand against you.**

Surround yourself with people full of faith, who believe in the promises of God, and who are advancing forward into the life He has called them to. Don't settle, and don't quit. Keep moving forward in faith, trusting that God is able to fulfill **every promise** He has made. You are called to **conquer**.

The Briefing Room

Step Eleven - Continue

Take one minute to think and write down the giants you are facing. See them as defeated foes. Maybe write down some of the truths in God's Word against those things holding you back. Continue to take a step forward, believing by faith that the war has already been won and you are already victorious.

GLORY DAYS

CHAPTER TWELVE

Every December in my house is chaotic—it's my birthday, my daughter's birthday (on the same day as mine!), and then Christmas is around the corner. Imagine those last two weeks of December at my house. My daughter is getting spoiled by her grandparents (I'm forgotten about now), and we are putting gifts under the tree for family and friends. So, my wife is ordering from Amazon on a daily basis, which is such a great joy for me. I am thrilled to get home to boxes and boxes of our money being well spent. I love you, babe.

Last year, our garage was packed with so many boxes and gifts after two weeks of birthdays, Christmas, and everything else Diana ordered. It was so cluttered that I couldn't find anything. One morning early in January, I went in to find my toolbox to build a toy for Aria, only to find myself in a maze of boxes and papers. I had delayed cleaning out the garage until the first few days of the new year, only to find myself trapped by bubble wrap, Ikea boxes, and Amazon package leftovers.

As I stood there looking at the mess, I thought about how our lives can sometimes feel the same—so full of distractions that it's hard to see where God is.

When life gets crowded and chaotic, it becomes difficult to see God's vision clearly. Today's fast-paced world keeps us busy—our schedules are packed, our minds are full, and our hearts are overwhelmed by anxiety, pressures, and responsibilities. When our lives are overly full, we lose sight of God's vision for us. We may be consumed with managing the day-to-day, leaving no room for God's purpose to shine through.

The Bible says, *"Where there is no vision, the people perish"* (Proverbs 29:18). Without vision, we are left without direction. If we don't know where we're going, we're prone to wander aimlessly, leading to destructive choices. That's why having a vision for our lives is so important—it keeps us grounded and aligned with what God wants for us.

We see a similar thing happening in the book of Habakkuk in the Bible. In Chapter 2 we see that Habakkuk is having a hard time seeing. Habakkuk 2:1-2 says, "*I will take my stand at my watch post and station myself on the tower, and look out to see what He will say to me, and what I will answer concerning my complaint. And the Lord answered me: 'Write the vision; make it plain on tablets, so he may run who reads it. For still the vision awaits its appointed time; it hastens to the end—it will not lie. If it seems slow, wait for it; it will surely come, it will not delay.'*"

Habakkuk had been voicing his complaints to God and was now ready to wait and see how God would respond. In His reply, God reminds Habakkuk that His plans unfold according to His timetable, not ours. Even when things seem slow, God's vision will surely come to pass. Can you learn to thank God that He is in control, sovereign, and working behind the scenes, even when we can't see it?

In the following verses, God pronounces five "woes" upon the enemies of His people, emphasizing His ultimate justice. Then, in verse 13, He says, "*Is it not from the Lord of Hosts that people labor merely for fire, and nations weary themselves for nothing?*" In other words, all the pursuits of the nations—wealth, power, success—are ultimately meaningless if they are not aligned with God.

Then comes the promise in verse 14: "*For the earth will be filled with the knowledge of the glory of the Lord as the waters cover the sea.*" This is the vision God gives Habakkuk—a vision of His glory filling the entire earth. It's a promise that, despite all the chaos and injustice in the world, God's glory will ultimately reign.

What does it mean that God's glory will fill the earth? How do we experience that glory in our own lives? Like many of us, Habakkuk struggled to see God at work in the midst of difficulty. The Babylonians had destroyed his city, enslaved his people, and made life unbearable. In his frustration, Habakkuk cried out to God, asking where He was in all the chaos. Have you ever felt like that? Like God is silent in the midst of your mess?

The Importance of Vision

This brings us to the importance of getting a **clear vision** for our lives. Whether you're single or married, young or old, we all need to have a clear picture of where we're headed. **What kind of person do you want to become? What kind of spouse or parent? What legacy do you want to leave behind?** Having a vision guides your decisions and actions. Without it, you'll drift in any direction, potentially losing yourself along the way.

A clear vision brings clear direction. Even if you don't have the full picture yet, start by identifying the direction in which you want to move. Some of us are stuck because we haven't set a vision for our lives, and as a result, we're letting the busyness of life cloud our judgment.

When your life becomes overly crowded, your **vision** becomes **cloudy**. You may be busy, but are you busy with the right things? It's possible to have a life filled with quantity but lacking in quality. God doesn't just want us to accumulate more "stuff"—He wants us to live lives filled with **purpose** and His presence.

This is what the Apostle Paul was referring to in Ephesians 3:18-19, when he spoke about knowing the *"breadth, length, height, and depth"* of God's love (quantity) and being filled with the **fullness of God** (quality). God wants to fill our lives with His glory, His goodness, and His presence. He wants us to reflect His nature in all that we do.

Reflectors of Glory

We are created in God's image, as Genesis 1:26 reminds us, and we are meant to be His reflection on earth. The word "image" in Hebrew can be understood as a shadow or reflection of God. We are not God, but we are created to mirror His love, mercy, grace, and nature to the world around us.

Think of it like this: when you stand in the light, you cast a shadow. That shadow is not you, but it reflects your actions. Similarly, we are meant to reflect God's character and love. When He looks at us, He should see a reflection of Himself, as if we are mirrors of His glory. Our purpose is to represent God on earth, living out His nature in love, joy, peace, and kindness.

God's ultimate goal is to **restore His image in us**. When He looks at humanity, He wants to see us reflecting His glory. We are meant to be mirrors of God's love, grace, and truth. Our lives should point back to Him, showing the world what God's love truly looks like.

However, sin shattered that reflection. Like a broken mirror, sin has fractured our ability to perfectly reflect God's image. None of us are perfect, and every time we choose sin, we further damage the reflection of God in our lives. Instead of being clear mirrors of His love and grace, we walk around with shattered reflections—showing pride, ego, and brokenness.

But here's the good news: **God is in the business of restoration**. He specializes in taking shattered lives and putting the pieces back together. As we surrender to Him, He begins to restore His image in us. We are made whole again, not by our own efforts, but by His grace. And as He restores us, we once again become **mirrors of His glory**, reflecting His love and grace to the world around us.

As we move forward in our lives, let's strive to reflect God's image in everything we do. Let's make sure our lives are not just full of quantity but **overflowing with the quality** of God's love and presence. He has a vision for each of us, and it's a vision of **restoration, hope, and glory**.

Many of us today may feel like shattered mirrors. We carry the weight of things we've done, regrets, and mistakes that distort the reflection of God we were created to show. As John Calvin said, *"Man resembles Him, and in man, God's glory is contemplated as in a mirror."* We are meant to show God's glory, but the image is broken by sin.

The question is: **When people see us, do they see God?** At work, in the grocery store, in our homes—do our actions reflect His nature? Do we mirror His love, kindness, and mercy, or are we reflecting something else? How about when we're driving and someone cuts us off—are we reflecting God then, or just our frustration?

We were created to reflect God's image on Earth. We're like mirrors, meant to show His nature—His love, grace, and mercy—to everyone around us. But if you're sitting here today feeling like your mirror is shattered, and you don't see any reflection of God in your life, **know this**: God is in the business of **restoring broken mirrors**. He takes what is broken and makes it whole again.

That's why when we talk about "glory days," it's not just about the past. **God can restore your mirror today,** no matter how broken it is. Jesus came to heal, restore, deliver, and free us so that we can reflect His glory. He wants to bring us into a season of *new* glory days—not just reflecting on the past but moving forward into something new.

For some of us, if we want to reflect God's image again, we need to first release what's holding us back. **Pride, ego, hurt, betrayal**—whatever it is, we have to let it go.

What do you need to release? We often think of "glory days" as being in the past—those times we thought were the best days of our lives. But God is always up to something **new**. Maybe you've been holding onto a hurt, a past mistake, or even a past success that's keeping you from moving forward. God takes us from **glory to glory,** meaning our best days are not behind us. Let go of the past, whether it's good or bad, and trust that God has more for you ahead.

We are meant to be reflections of God, but many of us are walking around shattered. If your mirror is broken, God wants to repair it. You may feel like you're not living up to the reflection of God's image, but **He can restore you**. Just like a mirror, we reflect what we focus on. If we're focused on God, we'll reflect His love, mercy, and grace.

Look at the Cross

In the book of Exodus, there's a powerful story about how they built the temple, specifically the basin where priests would wash before entering the Holy of Holies. **The basin was made from the mirrors of women who ministered at the entrance of the tent.** Exodus 38:8 says, "*He made the basin of bronze and its stand of bronze, from the mirrors of the ministering women who ministered at the entrance of the tent of meeting.*" These mirrors, once used for vanity or self-reflection, were melted down to create something that would cleanse and purify before entering God's presence.

Imagine this: Priests, after slaughtering sacrifices, would be covered in blood and dirt. Before they could enter God's presence, they had to wash in a basin made from those mirrors.

As they washed, the water reflected their image—covered in blood and dirt—and they began to see their faces reflected in the water now being covered by bloody water. It was a reminder to them that the blood would also cover all their mess. There's power in the blood to remove our stains, shame and sin. This reminds us that **the mirror, which once reflected brokenness and sin, now reflects the cleansing power of God's grace**.

This is the beauty of God's grace—**He doesn't leave us broken**. When we come to Him with our shattered lives, He begins the process of healing and restoration. We serve a God who is in the business of making all things new. He wants to restore His image in you so that you can walk in the fullness of your calling and purpose.

Whatever it is that's been holding you back, **today is the day to let go**. Release the past, allow God to heal the broken pieces, and step into your glory days. God wants to take you from strength to strength, from **glory to glory**. Your best days are not behind you—they are ahead, as He restores you and fills you with His presence. **Let's move forward**, reflecting His love and goodness to the world.

Mirrors are fascinating because they can either help or harm us, depending on what we see in them. Some people, filled with pride, admire themselves in every reflective surface they pass. Others avoid mirrors, feeling shame or insecurity about their reflection. But here's the point: **When I talk about "looking," I'm not talking about obsessing over ourselves.** Instead, we need to **fix our eyes on Jesus**.

The mirror is not meant to keep us stuck in sin or shame. It's supposed to remind us of who we are **in Christ**. We've been washed, cleansed, and made new. When you look at yourself now, don't focus on your past mistakes or failures. Instead, see the person Jesus has redeemed and made whole. **You are a new creation in Him.**

2 Corinthians 3:18 says, "*And we all, with unveiled face, beholding the glory of the Lord, are being transformed into the same image from one degree of glory to another. For this comes from the Lord who is the Spirit.*" When we gaze upon Jesus, it's like looking in a mirror. As we focus on Him, **we are transformed to reflect His image more and more**. **What you behold, you become**. The more you fix your eyes on Jesus, the more you are changed into His likeness.

As you behold Jesus, you will be transformed from the inside out. This transformation is like a **metamorphosis**, changing you into a new creation. Don't just hear the truth—live it out. Let your life reflect the image of God in every area.

A New Glory

You are not meant to live in brokenness or shame. **Jesus came to restore what was shattered**, and today, He wants to make you new. When you look in the mirror, don't see your flaws—see the person Christ has redeemed. You are being transformed from **glory to glory**, and the best is yet to come.

In ancient times, mirrors were made from sand. The process involved heating the sand at incredibly high temperatures to burn off impurities. Similarly, we are made from dust, and **God often takes us through the fire to purify and shape us**. The craftsmen would then shape the molten sand and coat it with a reflective material so that the glass would become a mirror.

In the same way, **God is shaping and refining us**—removing impurities, shaping us into His image, and restoring our ability to reflect His glory to the world.

In much the same way that a mirror maker shapes glass, the Holy Spirit works in us. He takes what was once ruined and shattered by sin and puts us through a process of sanctification—transforming us from the inside out. Just as a craftsman carefully molds glass into a mirror, **God shapes us,** forming us into reflections of His glory. When we are covered in His presence and anointed with His Spirit, we become ***mirrors that reflect His grace, love, and power to the world***.

Habakkuk 2:14 declares, "*For the earth will be filled with the knowledge of the glory of the Lord as the waters cover the sea.*" This is a promise we can trust, no matter how difficult or unclear life seems—***His glory will be revealed***.

We are called to be mirrors that reflect God's glory. The question is: **Will we choose to be part of that reflection?** Will we release the pride, ego, sin, and shame that hold us back and allow ourselves to be transformed into His image? God promises that one day, His glory will fill the earth. Whether we choose to participate or not, **His glory will prevail**—but we have the incredible opportunity to be a part of that reflection.

As you reach the end of this book, ask yourself: **Am I willing to be a mirror that reflects His glory?** Will I let go of my past and step into the new identity God has given me? God desires to restore you, to make you whole, and when you allow Him to do so, you become part of His divine plan to fill the earth with His glory.

A War Worth Fighting

There is a war, and there is an enemy lurking both within and without. Life may have shattered, bruised, and mauled us, but **that is not the end of the story**. God is not finished with you. On the contrary, **you are destined to win** this battle.

The enemy would love for you to believe that your brokenness is permanent and that the shattered pieces of your life cannot be mended. But **God is a master at taking broken pieces and creating something beautiful**.

I pray that the words in this book have inspired you to believe that **this is a war worth fighting**. It's a war for your soul, for your future, for your identity. And it's a war **you are destined to win**. In God's hands, you are being shaped into a reflection of His glory, and **nothing can stop His plan for your life**.

The Briefing Room

Step Twelve - Conquer

Take one minute to realize that Jesus has conquered every foe. Because of the Holy Spirit in you, that means you have won the war and you can conquer as well. Now allow the Holy Spirit to fill your life daily, every moment, with His power, and walk full of the fruits and gifts He gives, displaying the glory of God to the world around you. The battle is God's; the war is decided.

AFTERWORD

Did you notice how cleverly Alex Sagot devised his strategy in writing this book? One minute, he is taking you on a whirlwind tour of one of the world's most beautiful cities; the next minute, he is regaling you with stories of his childhood and youth. Then, before you know it, he is confronting you with the claims of Christ. As the book begins, the glamour of South Beach gives way to the hopelessness of the poverty "across the bridge." And before we know it, we've been summoned to engage in a spiritual war we didn't even know existed.

Several thoughts occurred to me as I read this book. I'll start with a statement Alex quoted: "Your life will always move in the direction of your strongest thoughts." There are all sorts of crazy ideas circulating about spiritual warfare, and people wind up running around addressing various demonic entities hovering over their cities. However, Paul sees things differently. As Alex notes correctly, the battle is always in the mind. In Greek, the word "mind" is not just our intellect but is closely related to the idea of the heart or the soul. That's why Paul speaks of the need for our mind to be transformed. What we think comes out of who we are. If our identity is not firmly rooted in Christ, our thinking will be seriously out of line with reality. And we see this all around us in our crazy culture today.

But Paul tells us something else that is profoundly encouraging. Where he speaks of this battle in 2 Corinthians 10, he uses the language of siege warfare. We often see ourselves as desperately trying to defend ourselves against the attacks of a powerful enemy, but the truth is we are on the offense, not the defense. We are laying siege victoriously to the strongholds of Satan.

How we do this goes back to the idea of what enables those strong thoughts that direct our lives. And that is the power of the Holy Spirit. Alex talks about the wrong windows we are looking through. He discusses the addictive power of social media and how that can backfire on us. He also addresses the distractions of life leading us down wrong paths.

What is the way out? How do we get off the defense and onto the offense? Too many Christians lapse into moralism, which then leads to defeat. Too often, preaching is reduced to a series of admonitions of what to do and what not to do. But the only real way to control our thoughts, our minds, and our lives is to hand them over daily to the Holy Spirit. That's why Paul tells us (in the Greek continuous present tense), "Be repeatedly, daily, continually filled with the Spirit" (Eph. 5:18). We can't produce the fruit of the Spirit any more than we can manufacture the gifts of the Spirit. All those wonderful things—love, joy, patience, and so on—are the fruit of the Spirit. The discipline Alex talks about can only be fueled by the Spirit.

What then is our responsibility? It is simply to offer ourselves in obedience. Of all his letters, Romans is the one Paul packs to the brim with doctrine. Have you ever noticed how, at the very beginning and the very end of the letter, he uses the phrase "the obedience of faith"? In Greek, the phrase means obedience is faith and faith is obedience. That's our part. The rest is up to God. How to follow everything else described in Romans, the entire Christian life in fact, is summed up in that one phrase. We obey in faith, and God empowers our obedience.

That's how we get to the reset Alex speaks of. That's how we get rid of the idols he warns us about in a society just as full of idols as there are gods in any other religion that has ever existed.

But all of this has a goal, a purpose. Alex points us to Paul's reference to a race. I taught at the Bible College in Athens several years ago. Right outside the college was a statue of a runner in the middle of a four-lane road. When I asked about it, I was told it was the exact midpoint of the road between Marathon and Athens, a distance of just over 26 miles. The runner was Pheidippides (don't call your kid that!), who brought the good news of the great victory at Marathon to the people of Athens.

Paul actually compares our life to a race several times. A race implies a goal. And that is where Alex leads us. The race is not just about the past, what we have conquered, or how far we have come. It's about the future, where we are going.

And this is where the book, as it should, ends. It ends, in fact, just where the Bible ends — in the glory of God. My mother-in-law recently had cataracts removed. Her first comment was, "It's so bright I can hardly see." Becoming a Christian takes us from darkness into light. What we begin to see is the glory of God. And as we behold Him, we are changed, Paul tells us, from one degree of glory to another, as we reflect His glory. We come into our destiny as image bearers of God. And so incredibly, when people see us, they see God. Not perfectly, of course, but genuinely. It's time to release the past and take hold of the glory.

This book is a short but powerful primer on how to encounter the glory of God in our lives today. We live those lives in the midst of the challenges and opportunities of a fallen world. But the message of this book is clear: God is with us, and He can do anything through us if only we surrender to Him. This is a book not just to read but to re-read, and then to pass on to others. It's a book forged in the experience of life by a man I know, love, and honor. The Biblical truths contained in this book will change your life if you live by them. They'll make you into the man or woman God wants you to be as His bearers of light in this dark world.

To God alone be the glory.

David Campbell

Professor, Theos University

Made in the USA
Middletown, DE
18 November 2024